DATE DUE

D1416952

LEUKEMIA

Other titles in Diseases and People

—Diseases and People—

LEUKEMIA

Alvin and Virginia Silverstein
and Laura Silverstein Nunn

 Enslow Publishers, Inc.
40 Industrial Road   PO Box 38
Box 398   Aldershot
Berkeley Heights, NJ 07922   Hants GU12 6BP
USA   UK
http://www.enslow.com

Acknowledgments
The authors would like to thank hematologist Dr. Peter Zauber and factchecker Monica Kaiser for their many helpful comments and suggestions.

Library of Congress Cataloging-in-Publication Data

Silverstein, Alvin.
    Leukemia / Alvin and Virginia Silverstein, Laura Silverstein Nunn.
       p. cm. — (Diseases and people)
    Includes bibliographical references and index.
    Summary: Gives a history of the study of leukemia; presents information
about its symptoms, causes, diagnosis, treatment, prevention, and social
and economic impact; and describes current research and future prospects.
    ISBN 0-7660-1310-3
    1. Leukemia—Juvenile literature. [1. Leukemia. 2. Diseases.]
    I. Silverstein, Virginia B. II. Nunn, Laura Silverstein. III. Title. IV. Series.
RC643.S54   2000
616. 99 ' 419—dc21
                                       99-050698

Printed in the United States of America

10 9 8 7 6 5 4 3

To Our Readers: We have done our best to make sure all Internet addresses in this book were active and appropriate when we went to press. However, the author and the publisher have no control over and assume no liability for the material available on those Internet sites or on other Web sites they may link to. Any comments or suggestions can be sent by e-mail to comments@enslow.com or to the address on the back cover.

Illustration Credits: American Cancer Society, pp. 44, 47; Barbara Kennedy, p. 77; CORBIS/Annie Griffiths Belt, p. 80; CORBIS/David Samuel Robbins, p. 71; © Corel Corporation, p. 66; courtesy of the National Childhood Cancer Foundation, pp. 11, 27; DíAMAR Interactive Corp., p. 87; Dr. Lance Liotta Library, National Cancer Institute, p. 41; Enslow Publishers, Inc., p. 36; G. Terry Sharrer, PhD., National Museum of American History, courtesy of the National Cancer Institute, p. 101; Los Angeles Times, © 1993, p. 52; Martha Swope © Time Inc., p. 8; National Cancer Foundation, p. 27; National Cancer Institute, pp. 62, 99; National Cancer Institute, photo by Bill Branson, p. 57; National Library of Medicine, pp. 15, 18, 21, 33; National Marrow Donor Program®, pp. 84, 94, 95.

Cover Illustration: National Cancer Institute, photo by Bill Branson.

Contents

LEUKEMIA

What is it? A cancer of the blood-forming tissues, resulting in the presence of large numbers of abnormal, immature white blood cells (leukocytes) and a decrease in red blood cells (erythrocytes). Types include lymphocytic and myelocytic; either can be acute (severe and rapidly progressing) or chronic (milder and long-term).

Who gets it? Both sexes, although it is more common in males. All races, although it is more common in whites than in blacks. Both adults and children. Although children account for less than 10 percent of new cases, leukemia kills more children than any other disease.

How do you get it? It is not contagious and is caused mainly by environmental factors such as exposure to radiations or chemicals. Genetic factors play a role, and viruses may cause some forms of leukemia.

What are the symptoms? Tiredness, weakness, pale skin, frequent infections, bruising easily, excessive bleeding from cuts, swollen abdomen.

How is it treated? Chemotherapy with drugs that kill rapidly dividing cells or stop their growth; radiation therapy of bone marrow with transplant of marrow or "cord blood" (from the umbilical cords and placentas of newborns) to replace killed cells.

How can it be prevented? By reducing exposure to environmental carcinogens and radiations, through community and global efforts, and by minimizing medical uses of radiations and protecting bone marrow during diagnostic X-ray procedures.

1

Blood Cells Gone Wild

Shelley Bruce had a very exciting childhood. She appeared in more than fifty TV commercials. In 1973, at age seven, she made her movie debut as an extra in *The Godfather*; and in 1978, she played the title role in the Broadway musical *Annie*. Shelley had always been a very active person, but when she was fifteen, her life changed suddenly.

Shelley had not been feeling like her usual energetic self for a while, when one day in early October 1981, she felt so ill that she went to see the school nurse. Shelley had a slight fever, and the nurse sent her home. When she woke up the next day, Shelley felt fine. The day after that, however, she had a fever again. Shelley was concerned and went to her doctor, who gave her a little finger-stick blood test. The test showed that her hemoglobin (the oxygen-rich protein in the blood) was

Shelly Bruce as Annie (right) appears on Broadway in 1978. With her are Reid Shelton as Daddy Warbucks, and Sandy, the dog.

low, which would explain why she was feeling so tired and having trouble breathing. Shelley's body was not getting enough oxygen.

Shelley was tired all the time and had hardly enough energy to do anything except lie down and watch television. Fever and extreme tiredness are typical of mononucleosis ("mono"), an infectious disease caused by a virus. Shelley's blood test had shown some abnormal white blood cells, which can also be a sign of mono. So Shelley's doctor ordered another blood test to check for mono. Four days later, however, the doctor called to say that the test had shown more abnormal white blood cells, which might indicate leukemia. Shelley and her family were in shock. In fact, Shelley couldn't even say the word *leukemia* for a week or so.

Diagnostic testing was begun right away. The doctor removed some bone marrow, the spongy material inside one of the large bones where the body's blood cells are produced. They studied the sample to find out what form of leukemia Shelley had. It was acute lymphocytic leukemia, the most common type in children. A sample of the fluid around Shelley's spinal cord was also examined to make sure the disease had not spread to the central nervous system.

After the diagnosis, Shelley received chemotherapy (treatment with drugs to kill cancer cells) and radiation treatments to help destroy the cancerous bone marrow cells. Shelley's body was weakened from all the treatments and was very susceptible to infections. Even a cold could be dangerous. She had to stay away from large groups of people, who could make her sick. Fortunately the treatments were successful. Several months later, Shelley showed no signs of the disease.[1]

In 1960, a popular textbook on childhood cancer described leukemia as "incurable." In those days, unhappy endings were typical, but tremendous progress has been made in treating the disease since then. By the time Shelley Bruce was diagnosed, medical treatments were already saving about

65 to 75 percent of young people with leukemia. Today, most cases of leukemia are considered to be treatable. Although some types of leukemia are more serious than others, many people with this disease really do survive. In most cases of childhood leukemia, the diagnosis does not have to be an automatic death sentence.

Leukemia is not a single disease. It includes a number of different kinds of cancers that start in the blood-forming tissues of the bone marrow found in the spaces inside the large bones. In leukemia, the body's white blood cells, or leukocytes, have essentially "gone wild."

The white blood cells are normally an important part of the body's system for fighting disease. In a person with leukemia, however, the total number of white blood cells increases enormously. In fact, the term *leukemia* comes from Greek words meaning "white (*leuko*) blood (*hemia*, or *emia*)." The white blood cells in leukemia are abnormal and unable to work effectively. As a result, a person with leukemia is defenseless against many common infections that someone with normal white blood cells can easily fight off.

The blood of a person with leukemia is abnormal in other ways, too. Along with an increased number of white blood cells, there are far fewer red blood cells than usual. Red blood cells carry oxygen to the body cells. In leukemia, there are so few red blood cells that cells all over the body do not get enough oxygen, which is needed to generate energy for the cells' activities. As a result, the person feels weak and tired. The numbers of blood platelets, a part of the blood that helps

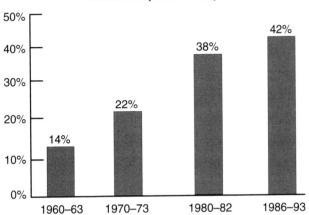

All Ages Survival Rates (5-Year)
Leukemia (1960–1993)

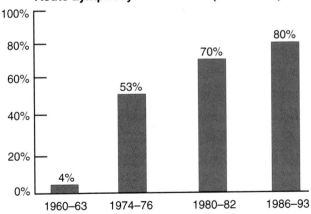

Childhood Survival Rates (5-Year)
Acute Lymphocytic Leukemia (1960–1993)

These charts show the dramatic increase in survival rates, both for leukemia in all age groups (top) and for leukemia in children under the age of fifteen (bottom). The statistics were compiled by the Leukemia Society of America.

clotting, are also reduced, which can lead to easy bruising and excessive bleeding.

Scientists are not sure exactly what causes leukemia; however, certain factors in the environment seem to increase the risk of developing it. For instance, exposure to radiation is one factor. Many people who were exposed to the radiation given off by the two atomic bomb explosions in World War II later developed leukemia. Early X-ray machines also increased the risk of leukemia. People exposed to certain toxic chemicals and waste materials may be at risk as well. Viruses might also be involved.

One of the main methods of treatment for leukemia is chemotherapy, or using drugs, to kill the abnormal white blood cells. Unfortunately, most chemicals that are poisonous enough to do that job also kill many normal cells. As a result, the patient may suffer from side effects, such as hair loss, nausea and vomiting, and loss of appetite.

Another way to kill diseased bone marrow cells is to destroy them with radiation. However, a person cannot live without bone marrow cells because blood cells constantly wear out and are replaced by new ones produced in the bone marrow. So the radiation, which kills good bone marrow cells as well as the diseased ones, is generally combined with a transplant of bone marrow donated by someone who does not have leukemia. This procedure replaces good bone marrow in the patient. The bone marrow donor's body tissues should be compatible with those of the patient. However, researchers have recently developed new techniques that greatly increase the number of suitable donors.

Although tremendous progress has been made, many people still die from leukemia. Researchers are actively working to learn the causes of the disease and to find better ways of treating it. They are searching for more specific drugs that can zero in precisely on cancer cells without harming normal ones. In addition, new techniques of gene therapy are being developed to correct the genetic misinformation that causes bone marrow cells to form leukemic white blood cells.

Experts recommend that the best way for leukemia patients and their families to cope is to learn as much as possible about the disease and what types of treatments are available. Education can provide a great deal of support and hope for the future.

2

Leukemia in History

Growing up in nineteenth-century Poland, Maria Sklodowska was determined to learn and succeed in a "man's world." After working for years to put her sister through medical school, she moved to Paris in 1891 to continue her own education. After earning a degree in physics, she fell in love with a young chemist, Pierre Curie. They were married in 1895 and formed a working partnership that ultimately made Marie Curie the world's most famous woman scientist. Together, the Curies studied the natural radiation given off by radioactive substances. While studying uranium ore, they discovered two highly radioactive elements, radium and polonium. To observe the effects of radium, Pierre tested it on his own skin. The radium burned his skin and made a wound.[1] Marie herself had burns on her fingertips from handling radium. Though the effects of radium proved very powerful, these scientists were not aware of the possible dangers associated with the radioactivity that was given off by the element. As a result, they took very few precautions while they were handling chemicals and radioactive substances.

In 1903, Marie and Pierre Curie won a Nobel Prize in physics for their discovery of the radioactive elements. They shared the prize with French physicist Antoine Henri Becquerel, who had discovered the natural radioactivity of the element uranium. Marie Curie became the first woman to win a Nobel Prize.

In 1906, Pierre Curie died suddenly when he was hit by a horse-drawn cart. Marie Curie was heartbroken but was

This drawing by André Castaigne shows Marie and Pierre Curie (center and right) experimenting with the element radium.

determined to continue the work that she and her husband had started together. In 1911, Marie Curie won another Nobel Prize, this time in chemistry for isolating pure radium and studying its chemical properties.

By the late 1920s, the continued exposure to the high-energy radiation she worked with was finally taking its toll on Marie Curie. She was greatly weakened and almost blind. In 1934, she died of leukemia at the age of sixty-six. Strangely, during all the time that Marie studied radioactive properties, she never really made a connection between the effects of radium exposure and the illnesses of her husband, her assistants, and herself. (Pierre Curie had felt tired and weak and suffered from a series of illnesses for years before his death.

Helping Soldiers with Science

In 1914, during World War I, Marie Curie found a way to use her scientific knowledge to help injured soldiers. Pictures taken using X rays could locate shrapnel and bullets lodged in a person's body and give important information about the patient's condition. Curie set up X-ray vans so that the wounded people did not have to be moved. She also helped to provide X-ray equipment for hospitals. She trained about one hundred fifty women to operate the machines. At that time, however, the only protection people had from the radiation was a metal screen and fabric gloves, which were not very effective.[2]

Their daughter, Irène Joliot-Curie, and son-in-law, Frédéric Joliot-Curie, who continued Marie's work and also won a Nobel Prize, both died of leukemia as well.) Marie's notebooks, in which she recorded all of her findings, are still in existence today—but they are locked up because they are too radioactive to handle![3]

The causes of leukemia were virtually unknown when Marie Curie was doing her work on radioactivity. The disease itself, however, had been recognized about fifty years before she began her career.

The Discovery of a "New" Disease

Leukemia has probably been around for thousands of years. It was not until the 1800s, however, that it was finally described as a distinct disease.

In 1827, a very strange medical case intrigued French physician Alfred Velpeau. A sixty-three-year-old man had become ill; he had a swollen abdomen, was running a fever, and was very weak. Shortly after he was admitted to the hospital, the man died. Dr. Velpeau, who had been caring for this man, did an autopsy (a postdeath physical examination) to find out what caused his death. The patient had a very large liver and spleen. In fact, the spleen weighed about 10 pounds (about 4.5 kilograms). It was about twenty times its normal size! The man's blood had a strange appearance. It was pale, thin, and mixed with pus. Dr. Velpeau did not realize it at the time, but his notes provided the first accurate description of a leukemia case. This mysterious case intrigued other doctors, who used Dr. Velpeau's description as a guide for future cases with similar circumstances.[4]

More than a decade later, two other French physicians, Drs. Barth and Donne, reported on some more cases of leukemia. When Dr. Barth performed an autopsy on a forty-four-year-old woman in 1839, he found that she had an enlarged spleen and, after careful examination, noticed that she had pus in her blood, just as in Dr. Velpeau's case. Dr. Donne viewed the woman's blood under a microscope and found that more than half the blood cells were white blood

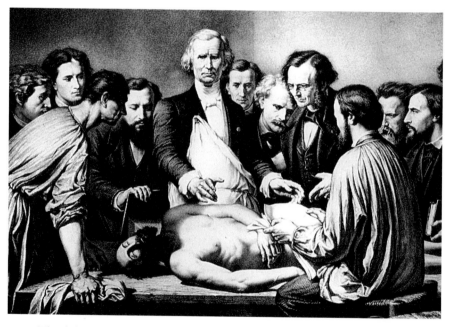

This lithograph by Louis Eugene Pirodon shows Alfred Velpeau giving an anatomy lesson to his students. Velpeau (center) uses a dead body, or cadaver, to demonstrate how the human body functions, and to try to determine the dead man's cause of death.

cells. In 1844, Dr. Donne reported on several other patients who probably had leukemia as well.[5]

In 1845, reports were published by two physicians in Scotland describing similar cases. Dr. David Craigie noted that his patient had a greatly enlarged spleen and liver, and his blood contained globules of pus. The patient described by Dr. John Hughes Bennett also had an enlarged liver (11 pounds; 5 kg) an enlarged spleen (8 pounds; about 3.5 kg), and pus-filled blood. When Dr. Bennett studied the patient's blood under a microscope, he noticed an overwhelming number of white blood cells, as would be expected during an infection. But there were no signs of infection. Dr. Bennett did not realize that the "colorless globules" he saw were not normal white blood cells, and decided that "pus in the blood" was the cause of the patient's death.[6]

Later in 1845, the renowned German pathologist Dr. Rudolf Virchow became the first person to recognize that patients like these were all suffering from the same disease. In a published report, Dr. Virchow described a case similar to that of Dr. Bennett's. As in the previous cases mentioned, the blood of Dr. Virchow's patient appeared to be filled with pus. Normally, a person's blood contains many more red blood cells than white blood cells. Dr. Virchow noticed that in this patient's blood there were many white blood cells but very few red blood cells. As a result, Dr. Virchow described the disease as "white blood" or *weisses blut* in German. Later, he changed the name to leukemia, from two Greek words also meaning "white blood."[7]

Rudolf Virchow was also the first person to describe two major kinds of leukemia. He called one kind splenic leukemia because it seemed to affect the spleen. (Today this kind is called myelogenous leukemia.) The other type he called lymphatic leukemia because it seemed to affect the lymph nodes, the masses of glandlike tissue found along the lymph vessels, especially in the neck, groin, and armpits. Still, Virchow could not be sure if the white blood cells in the two types of the disease were different from the white blood cells in healthy people, or if there were just more white cells.[8]

In 1890, German scientist Paul Ehrlich discovered that there are actually several kinds of white blood cells. Ehrlich was able to distinguish the white blood cells by staining them with special aniline dyes. Under the microscope, he could also see the inner structures of the cells that could not be seen before. Ehrlich found out that when myeloid cells (white blood cells produced in the bone marrow) become abnormal, they accumulate in the spleen and liver, as well as in other organs and tissues. This discovery fits Virchow's description of splenic or myelogenous leukemia.[9] Another type of white blood cells, called lymphocytes, were later found to be associated with Virchow's other type of leukemia, lymphatic leukemia (also called lymphocytic leukemia).

Doctors noticed that some leukemia cases were more serious than others. People who died quickly, within a few weeks to a few months, were considered to have acute leukemia. People who lived with leukemia for at least several years had chronic leukemia.

German pathologist Rudolph Virchow was one of the first scientists to identify leukemia. He first described the disease as *weisses blut*, which is German for "white blood."

A Positive Outlook

Scientists continued to learn more about leukemia. Unfortunately, no matter how much was discovered about this "new" disease, the diagnosis was still the same—a virtual death sentence. Everyone who had leukemia eventually died from it. In fact, with no hope for survival, many doctors thought it was wrong to tell patients that they had the disease.

Research conducted during the early 1900s brought the first hope for leukemia patients. Ironically, this hope came about as an indirect result of research efforts to produce new weapons for chemical warfare during World War I. While studying the effects of extracts from mustard plants on experimental animals, Paul Ehrlich discovered some very poisonous compounds. Other German scientists continued his work and produced mustard gas, which was used in the war. It was not a very useful weapon, though, because winds often blew the poisonous gas back on the German soldiers.

Doctors performed autopsies on the victims and discovered that mustard gas had damaged their bone marrow and lymph nodes. These findings were reported in 1919 but were ignored until another World War revived interest in chemical weapons. In 1942, scientists at Yale University tried to use nitrogen mustard as a form of chemotherapy for lymph node cancers (lymphomas). Controlled doses of the poisons produced dramatic improvement, first in mice and then in a human patient with lymphoma. Other researchers in the United States and in London continued these studies using chemically related compounds and eventually developed effective treatments for chronic leukemia.[10]

In 1948, a huge breakthrough was made in leukemia treatment. Scientists found that a vitamin called folic acid could activate the production of leukemia cells. At Lederle Laboratories in the United States, researchers made compounds that were very similar to folic acid but different enough so that if the cancerous white blood cells picked up these compounds in the blood instead of the true folic acid, they could not use the compounds in producing new leukemia cells. Growth of the cancer would thus be stopped. This discovery was tested on sixteen patients with acute leukemia at Boston Children's Hospital. Ten of these patients showed major signs of improvement. Using similar approaches, scientists developed new drugs, and the outlook for leukemia patients gradually improved. In fact, over the next twenty years, many patients with acute leukemia were living for more than five years after their diagnosis.[11]

In 1968, the future got even brighter for leukemia patients when the first bone marrow transplant was performed successfully at the University of Minnesota.[12] This technological advance was especially encouraging for patients who could not be helped by chemotherapy and other treatments.

3

What Is Leukemia?

In 1860 in Würzberg, Germany, five-year-old Maria Speyer had done very well during her first year of kindergarten. In her second year, however, things seemed to change. Maria no longer paid attention in class, and she failed to do her assignments. Maria had always been bright and enthusiastic, but now she was tired and uncooperative. Her mother was scheduled to speak to the teacher about her daughter's lack of motivation the next day.

That night, however, while Maria's mother was giving her two daughters a bath, she noticed some disturbing red splotches on Maria's arms, legs, and body.

The next day, instead of going to the conference with Maria's teacher, Mrs. Speyer took both her daughters to see their family doctor, Dr. Stern. For weeks, Maria's younger sister Eva had been feeling ill, but it had not seemed serious. Now, with both children showing symptoms, a doctor's visit seemed urgent.

Dr. Stern was very concerned about the various "blood spots" and bruises on Maria's skin. In fact, more marks had appeared since the previous day. Both Maria and Eva had enlarged spleens, but Maria's spleen was enormous, nearly filling the left side of her abdomen. Dr. Stern could not make a diagnosis yet, but he thought the girls' illnesses were probably contagious. He told them to stay home, and he prescribed cod liver oil to rid their bodies of poisons. Eva soon improved, but Maria did not. In fact, she had gotten worse: She was hot and irritable, had more bruises, and was too weak to get out of bed. She slept most of the day; when she was awake, she complained that her head hurt and her neck was stiff.

Confused by Maria's condition, Dr. Stern called Dr. D. Biermer, a physician who was well informed about the latest medical research and might be able to shed some light on the situation. Dr. Biermer took blood from Maria and examined it under the microscope, a new tool in medicine at that time. After studying the structure of Maria's blood and reviewing her various symptoms—anemia (a lowered red blood cell count), weakness, an enlarged spleen and liver, an enlarged heart, possible pneumonia, and bruising in the skin—Dr. Biermer had a diagnosis. Maria had leukemia. Dr. Biermer explained that Maria's case was similar to a deadly illness that had been described in the late 1840s, but no one had ever reported leukemia in a child before. Thus, Maria Speyer became the first reported case of childhood leukemia. Unfortunately, not long after the diagnosis, Maria died. Dr. Stern soon scheduled an autopsy so Maria's body could be studied and more could be learned about how leukemia affects all the various parts of the body.[1]

Who Gets Leukemia?

Leukemia is often thought of as primarily a childhood disease. That is probably because leukemia kills more children under fifteen years of age than any other disease. However, leukemia actually occurs in many more adults than it does in children; more than half of all leukemia cases develop in people over the age of sixty.

In 1998, approximately 140,000 people in the United States were living with leukemia. An estimated 28,700 new cases of leukemia were expected to be diagnosed during that year, with only 2,200 of these cases affecting children under the age of fifteen. In that year, an estimated 21,600 Americans would die of leukemia.[2]

Leukemia can strike anyone anywhere in the world and at any age. Certain groups of people, however, seem to have a higher rate than other groups. In the United States, leukemia is more common in white people than in blacks. Leukemia also tends to occur more often in males than in females. Children with chromosome abnormalities such as Down syndrome, Bloom syndrome, or Fanconi aplastic anemia have an increased risk of developing leukemia. (Nevertheless, most people with these conditions will not develop leukemia.)[3]

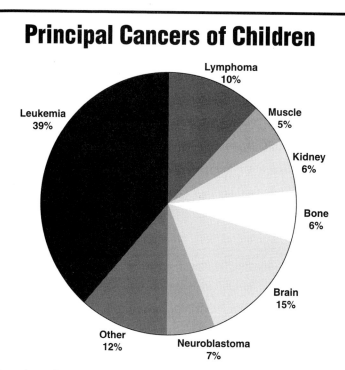

Principal Cancers of Children

- Lymphoma 10%
- Muscle 5%
- Kidney 6%
- Bone 6%
- Brain 15%
- Neuroblastoma 7%
- Other 12%
- Leukemia 39%

This chart from the National Childhood Cancer Foundation shows the relative number of cases of cancers in children. Leukemia is the most widespread cancer in this group. However, children do not have the principal cancers found in adults: those of the breast, prostate, lung, and bowel.

What Are the Symptoms?

Leukemia is not an easy disease to diagnose. Many of the symptoms are similar to those of the common cold, the flu, mononucleosis, or some other illness. People often assume that a nagging illness is caused by some virus or bacteria, and it will eventually go away. But leukemia does not go away. Instead, the symptoms hang on and get worse. A combination of some of the typical symptoms could be a clue that something is really wrong. What should you look for?

- pale skin
- tiny red dots on the skin
- weakness
- constant tiredness
- loss of appetite
- high fever
- headaches
- irritability
- infection that never seems to go away
- pain in joints, back, legs
- bruising easily
- excessive bleeding from cuts, nose, or gums (blood does not clot)
- swollen lymph nodes in neck or groin
- swollen upper abdomen due to enlargement of spleen and/or liver

The kind and severity of the symptoms can vary greatly. Some people may have symptoms so mild that they are hardly noticeable. Others, however, may be in such pain that they cannot get out of bed. In some people, the symptoms may come and go. Without treatment, however, the symptoms will continue to worsen. A doctor should be contacted when symptoms are long-lasting or keep coming back.[4]

What Causes Leukemia?

Leukemia is a cancer of the blood-forming tissues. It is not contagious. It is not like a cold—you cannot catch leukemia by playing with a friend who has it. Leukemia is not inherited. If someone in your family has leukemia, that doesn't mean that you will develop it.

Although leukemia is not inherited, genetics most likely plays a role. For some reason, a genetic change occurs in a single white blood cell somewhere in the bone marrow. The cell with this mutant gene then reproduces itself uncontrollably. Scientists do not know exactly what causes this genetic change. What they do know, however, is that certain risk factors may increase the likelihood of developing leukemia.

Radiation exposure is probably the best-known factor that increases the risk of developing leukemia. High doses of radiation are more likely to cause leukemia than low doses of radiation. Marie Curie, her daughter, and son-in-law all died from leukemia because they did not protect themselves when handling highly radioactive elements. The additional radiation exposure from the X-ray equipment she worked with probably also contributed to Marie Curie's condition. Modern X-ray machines produce much lower doses of radiation than during Marie Curie's time. In addition, physicians are now very careful to protect their patients as well as themselves from any exposure to the radiation. These days, X-rays machines pose minimal risk for causing the development of cancer. However, most experts agree that X rays should not be administered unless it is absolutely necessary. The exposure to X rays that a person accumulates over the years could possibly increase the risk of later developing leukemia or some other cancer.

Some of the strongest evidence for a definite link between radiation exposure and leukemia comes from World War II, when atomic bombs were dropped on two cities in Japan, Hiroshima and Nagasaki. Atomic bomb survivors showed the effects of the radiation exposure when they died of leukemia some years later. Throughout Japan, there was a 50 percent increase in the leukemia rate from 1946 to the early 1950s. There was another sharp rise in 1959, following hydrogen bomb tests in the Pacific and Siberia that resulted in heavy radioactive fallout in Japan and contamination of the fish that were a large part of the Japanese diet.[5]

Certain chemicals may increase the risk of developing leukemia. For example, people who are exposed to large doses of benzene, a chemical used to manufacture medicines, dyes, artificial leather, and linoleum, among other products, have a risk ten times that of the general population. Numerous other carcinogens (cancer-causing chemicals) are also found in our environment and are believed to be a major cause of leukemia.

Smoking cigarettes, which is a well-known cause of a variety of cancers, has also been found to be a possible cause of an adult form of leukemia. Parents who constantly smoke around their children may be putting them at risk of developing leukemia or some other disease.

Viruses have been found to cause leukemia in cows, cats, chickens, mice, and gibbons. These animal viruses do not affect human cells. But recently, viruses called human T-cell

Does America's Favorite Food Cause Cancer?

We eat them at baseball games; we eat them at picnics. Even President Franklin D. Roosevelt once offered hot dogs to the King and Queen of England as a symbol of American culture. For years, though, nutritionists have been saying that hot dogs are bad for us—they contain a lot of fat, sodium, and chemical preservatives.

In 1994, researchers at the University of Southern California (USC) reported that eating large quantities of hot dogs may cause leukemia in children. The researchers found that children who ate twelve to twenty hot dogs each month were ten times more likely to develop leukemia than children who did not have a lot of hot dogs. Hot dogs contain nitrites, a chemical additive used to add flavor. When combined with other natural substances, nitrites have been known to cause cancer in animals. Today's nitrite-containing meats also contain vitamin C, which is supposed to counteract the bad effects of nitrites. But this addition may not help when large quantities of the meats are eaten.

Critics of the USC study say that the study does not prove anything. Eric Hentges, director of nutrition research for the National Live Stock and Meat Board, noted that the study did not indicate the subjects' other eating habits, or other environmental factors involved. In addition, foods such as ham, bacon, and sausage all contain nitrites, too, but the study found a link only between hot dogs and leukemia.[6]

leukemia/lymphoma viruses (HTLV), known to damage a
type of white blood cells called T cells, have been linked to a
rare form of leukemia in adults. Cases have been reported in
many parts of the world, from Japan, southern Italy, Africa,
and South America to the southeastern United States. While
the T-cell virus has been found in adults, no virus has so far
been found to cause leukemia in children.[7]

Genetic factors seem to be involved in some leukemia cases.
For instance, Down syndrome, which is caused by an abnor-
mality of the chromosomes, has been linked with an increased
risk of leukemia. Chromosomes contain information that
determines our inherited traits, such as eye and hair color, as
well as the production and functioning of cells. Normally, a
person has forty-six chromosomes, but a person with Down
syndrome has an extra chromosome. It is believed that this
extra chromosome somehow increases the likelihood of developing leukemia. A person with Down syndrome is up to
fifteen times more likely to develop leukemia than a person
without Down syndrome.[8]

In some cases, an abnormally short chromosome, called
the Philadelphia chromosome, has been linked to a rare form
of leukemia. It is believed that this genetic mutation causes
something to go wrong in cell development and function.[9]

More evidence of a strong link between genetic factors and
leukemia is provided by studies of leukemia in identical twins.
Researchers have discovered that under the same conditions, if
one twin has leukemia, the other has a 15 to 25 percent
increased risk of developing the disease, compared to the

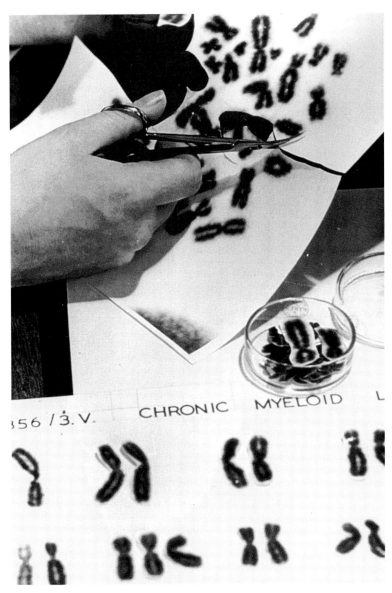

This researcher is cutting and sorting chromosomes for a study on various types of leukemia. Today this type of work is generally done by computer instead of by hand.

general population. It seems likely that genetics plays a large role in the increased risk, since fraternal twins, who share only half of their genetic inheritance, do not show a significant increased risk of developing leukemia. Both fraternal twins have leukemia less than one percent of the time.[10]

What Our Blood Does

Leukemia is a blood disorder. If we want to understand how leukemia develops, we need to understand the composition of our blood and what it does.

Beating the Odds

Although children with Down syndrome have a higher than normal risk of developing leukemia, researchers at the Barbara Ann Karmanos Cancer Institute in Detroit have found in one respect the odds are in their favor. In 1996 they reported that children with Down syndrome and acute myeloid leukemia (AML)—the deadliest form—are twice as likely to survive their disease as children (and adults) without Down syndrome.

The children with Down syndrome are ten times as sensitive to ara-C, the most effective chemotherapy drug for AML, as children without Down syndrome, so the same dose of the drug works much better. "Children with Down syndrome are unique," says cancer researcher Dr. Jeffrey Taub. "If we can identify how these children respond to the drug, then we may be able to mimic the process in patients without Down syndrome."[11] About three hundred fifty cases of AML in children are diagnosed each year, and 5 to 10 percent of them are in children with Down syndrome.

Blood is a complex mixture of chemicals and cells suspended in a watery fluid. It flows in a complex network of branching tubes (blood vessels) that go out from the heart to all parts of the body and back to the heart. This is called the circulatory system. As the blood circulates, it carries oxygen, nutrients, hormones, and other important chemicals to various parts of the body. It also removes waste products, such as carbon dioxide, from the body's cells. Blood also helps the lymphatic system fight infection.

The lymphatic system is closely associated with the circulatory system. Tiny blood vessels, called capillaries, have leaky walls, and some of the fluid from the blood these capillaries carry leaks out into the surrounding tissues. This fluid drains into the tiny vessels of the lymphatic system. The job of the lymphatic system is to get rid of any excess fluid from the tissues and put it back in the bloodstream. Along the vessels of the lymphatic system, there are the lymph nodes, clustered in certain places such as the neck, groin, underarms, pelvis, and abdomen. The lymph nodes contain disease-fighting cells that protect the body. The lymph nodes often become swollen when they are busy fighting an infection.

Three main kinds of solid particles are suspended in the watery fluid of the blood: red blood cells, platelets, and white blood cells. These cells are produced in the bone marrow, the spongy material that fills the spaces of the large bones. They all start out as stem cells, a primitive kind of blood-forming cell that can produce whatever kind of blood cell the body needs. Some stem cells, for example, divide to form erythroblasts. These are immature red blood cells, which divide and develop further to form mature red blood cells, or erythrocytes. (*Erythro* comes from the Greek word meaning "red." *Cyte* comes from a Greek word meaning "cell.")

Other stem cells take a different line of development. They may produce several kinds of leukocytes (white blood cells). These include lymphoblasts, which develop into several different kinds of mature forms called lymphocytes. Another group of white blood cells are formed when stem cells develop into myeloblasts, which differentiate further into myelocytes. (You may recall that *myelo* refers to the bone marrow.) Still other stem cells may develop into monoblasts, which form monocytes and macrophages, the white blood cells that gobble up and destroy invading germs.

The platelets are the third branch of the "tree" of blood cell lines. The stem cells that give rise to them form as very large cells which, after maturing, split up into fragments.

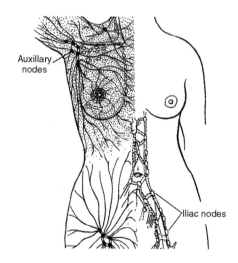

Auxillary
nodes

Iliac nodes

The lymphatic system is a network of vessels that carry the lymph, a clear fluid containing white blood cells that help fight infection and disease. Lymph nodes are scattered throughout the system. They help to filter the lymph fluid.

Red blood cells, or erythrocytes, are the most numerous of all the cells—25 trillion red blood cells circulate through an adult's body! A single drop of blood contains more than 250 million red blood cells. The average lifespan of a red blood cell is 120 days. Old, worn-out red cells are broken down in the liver and spleen, and their chemicals are recycled. Each second, from 2 to 10 million red blood cells in your body are destroyed, and an equal number of new red cells are produced by the bone marrow to replace them.

Each red blood cell contains a red pigment, called hemoglobin. Hemoglobin is a protein that picks up oxygen from the lungs and carries it to various parts of the body. Transporting oxygen is a very important job. Oxygen is needed for the energy-producing reactions that power all the body's activities. Each time you move a muscle, digest a meal, or even think, oxygen-using reactions supply the power for your actions.

Platelets are also called thrombocytes, which literally means "clotting cells." They are tiny, disk-shaped particles that form clots to stop bleeding. When platelets run into the edges of a damaged blood vessel, they become sticky. The platelets start to pile up until they form a plug that fills the hole. That stops the bleeding. Without platelets, we could bleed to death from a very small cut.

White blood cells, or leukocytes, help to protect the body from foreign invaders such as viruses and bacteria. Normally, there are only a small number of white blood cells circulating in the bloodstream—there are about seven hundred times more red blood cells than white blood cells. But during an infection, the body sends out a whole army of white blood cell soldiers to attack the foreign invaders. These cells can change their shape and squeeze between body cells to get to the site of injury, infection, or inflammation (swelling).

There are three main types of leukocytes, each with a special job to do:

Granulocytes make up about 70 percent of the white blood cells. The granulocytes seek out disease germs and destroy them by gobbling them up.

Monocytes make up only 3 to 4 percent of the white blood cells. They attack germs that the granulocytes did not catch. In an active infection, they can swell up into giant white cells called macrophages, each of which eats up as many as one hundred bacteria.

Lymphocytes can accumulate in the lymph nodes and other lymphoid tissues. The various kinds of lymphocytes are involved in recognizing and attacking foreign substances, whether they are invading germs or the body's own cells that have changed and become cancerous.

What Happens in Leukemia?

In leukemia, something goes wrong in the body's normal cell-producing mechanisms. The problem starts with defective stem cells. These cells produce immature white blood cells, called blasts. Unlike mature white blood cells, blasts lack the disease-fighting abilities and are defenseless against invading disease germs. Therefore, the body's defenses, the immune system, cannot function properly. As a result, a person with leukemia will get infections easily. The immune system may become so damaged that a normally mild illness can kill a person with leukemia.

Normally, healthy cells divide and make copies of themselves. They then grow in a patterned, controlled manner. But in leukemia, the abnormal white blood cells will divide, make copies of themselves, and multiply uncontrollably. Eventually, millions of abnormal white blood cells flood the bone marrow, stopping the growth of other stem cells. This causes a tremendous reduction in the number of normal white blood cells, red blood cells, and platelets. The blood becomes overrun by abnormal immature white blood cells.

A sharp decrease in oxygen-carrying red blood cells produces a condition called anemia. Anemia is typically associated with symptoms like paleness, tiredness, and weakness. Anemia is a common symptom of leukemia and occurs when there are not enough red blood cells to deliver oxygen to the various organs of the body.

A reduction of platelets in the blood can cause problems, too. Platelets are needed to close up wounds to stop the bleeding. People with leukemia often bruise easily and bleed excessively. For instance, some people may notice that their gums may start bleeding when they brush their teeth. Some may get red spots on their skin, especially on their arms and legs. Children who scrape their knees after falling off a bike may bleed more than usual. Excessive bleeding can make the body more vulnerable to infection.

When the leukemic cells spill out into the bloodstream,

they start to invade vital organs such as the lungs, kidneys, liver, spleen, and central nervous system. Leukemia patients often develop an enlarged spleen and liver, but other parts of the body may be harmed as well.[12]

Forms of Leukemia

The term *leukemia* does not describe a single disease, but rather a condition that comes in different forms. A combination of factors, including the patient's age, the type and severity of the symptoms, and the type of cells infected, are used to distinguish various forms of the disorder.

The two main types of leukemia are lymphocytic leukemia (also called lymphoblastic, lymphatic, or lymphoid leukemia) and myelocytic leukemia (also called myeloblastic, myeloid, myelogenous, or granulocytic leukemia).

Each type of leukemia comes in two different forms, acute and chronic. The acute form is an aggressive kind of cancer and develops very quickly, producing severe symptoms. Acute leukemias can cause death in a matter of weeks or months. The chronic form is milder than the acute form and develops more slowly, usually over a period of years. The patient may not have any obvious signs of the illness.

In *acute lymphocytic leukemia (ALL)*, there is an over-production of rapidly multiplying, immature lymphocytes. This is the most common form of leukemia that develops in children. In fact, it is often called childhood leukemia. It most commonly occurs in children between the ages of two and

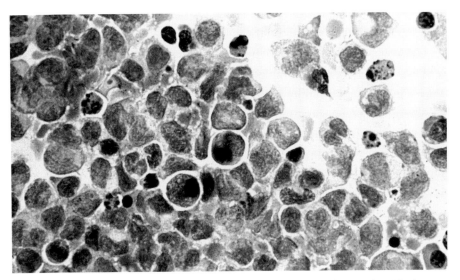

Human cells with acute myelogenous leukemia (AML) are identified under the microscope.

eight, but adults can also develop this form. It is also the most treatable form of leukemia.

In *chronic lymphocytic leukemia (CLL)*, there is an over-production of slowly multiplying, immature lymphocytes. This kind of white blood cell leaves the bone marrow and often invades the lymph nodes and spleen. CLL most commonly occurs in people over the age of fifty.

In *acute myelogenous leukemia (AML)*, there is an overproduction of rapidly multiplying, immature granulocytes. This form most commonly occurs in people over the age of forty.

Chronic myelogenous leukemia (CML) initially involves an overproduction of slowly multiplying granulocytes. This is a rare form of leukemia, especially in children. It is most commonly seen in adults between the ages of thirty and sixty.[13]

4

Diagnosing Leukemia

JoAnne Johnson was a hard-working honor student in high school. In 1988, eighteen-year-old JoAnne was very excited about starting her first year at Brown University. A couple of months into the school year, however, she suddenly started to feel tired all the time. Normally a strong, energetic person, she was spending a lot of time in bed, and even missed some classes.

JoAnne became concerned, especially when everyday activities suddenly became an enormous effort. In October 1988, while playing water polo at her new school, her muscles suddenly weakened—she hardly had enough strength to make it to the net at the other end of the pool or to lift her arms to hit the ball.

The previous day, JoAnne had gone to Health Services complaining about her recent lack of energy. After explaining to the nurse about her hectic schedule, which included several classes, political work, a part-time job, water polo, and volleyball, as well as a few dorm parties, the nurse exclaimed, "No wonder you're exhausted!" The nurse thought JoAnne's symptoms were probably nothing to worry about, but she took some of JoAnne's blood for testing, just in case. JoAnne had hoped it was nothing, but she was worried about the bruises on her skin. A month before, she had gotten a bruise on her hip after a little canoe accident, and the bruise did not fade— it just got darker and spread. She was also getting terrible splotches on her skin.

Only two days after JoAnne's blood was taken for testing, she received a call from Dr. Wheeler at Health Services. Her blood test results had come back, and she had to go down to the Health Center to see the doctor right away. JoAnne thought that maybe she was coming down with the flu, or maybe it was mononucleosis. When JoAnne arrived at the Health Center, Dr. Wheeler told her that she had an acute form of leukemia. Frightened, JoAnne asked, "Am I going to die?" Dr. Wheeler explained to JoAnne that leukemia can be treated. What Dr. Wheeler did not reveal, however, was her alarming white blood cell count (WBC)—it was 200,000, and 10,000 is normal. JoAnne needed treatment right away.

JoAnne went home to her family physician, Dr. Gootenberg, who would have access to the proper facilities. Before JoAnne could begin treatment, her doctor had to find out which white cells had become cancerous. That meant further testing. JoAnne had a bone marrow biopsy, in which a small sample of marrow from one of the large bones was removed with a hollow needle and examined under a microscope. A few days later, her doctor told her that she had a very rare and aggressive form of leukemia. Sadly, Dr. Gootenberg predicted that her chances did not look good. In the end, he was right. JoAnne lost her battle with leukemia sixteen months

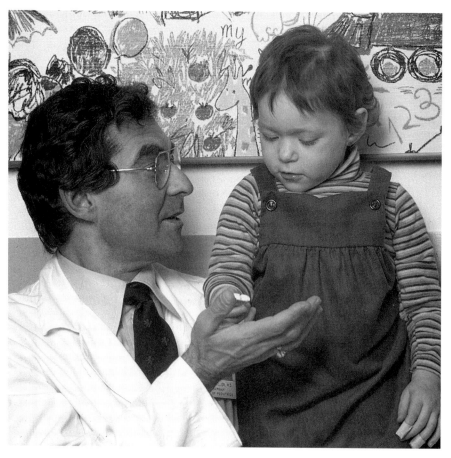

The first step in diagnosing leukemia, or any disease, is to have a complete physical examination by your doctor.

after the diagnosis was first made. She died before a suitable bone marrow donor could be found.[1]

Leukemia is very difficult to diagnose. Many of the early symptoms are similar to a variety of other illnesses. Some of the first signs of leukemia may include fever, paleness of skin, loss of appetite, tiredness, and weakness. These signs are often confused with those of the common cold, flu, mono, or some other illness. As was true in JoAnne's case, fatigue may seem like the logical product of a young person's busy life.

Unfortunately, it is easy to overlook the early symptoms of leukemia. However, a proper diagnosis should be made as soon as possible. It is very important to identify the type of white blood cell that has become leukemic, because each kind of leukemia requires slightly different treatment.[2] Leukemia patients have the best chances of surviving when they are correctly diagnosed early and can receive appropriate treatment before the disease has time to do more damage. For many patients, early detection can mean a positive outlook.

Laboratory Tests

The only way to get an accurate diagnosis of leukemia is through laboratory testing. The first diagnostic test for leukemia is a blood test. Sometimes, abnormal cells can be seen through a microscope, and a preliminary diagnosis of leukemia can be made. However, further chemical testing is usually needed. The most common routine laboratory test performed is the complete blood count (CBC) test. The CBC test measures the amounts of different types of cells in the

Collecting Information

Do you have a cold that does not seem to go away? Or maybe the "cold" seems to come and go. It's time to see the doctor. Any illness that sticks around for more than a couple of weeks is usually serious enough to warn you that something is wrong.

The doctor will need to collect information about the patient. What are the symptoms? Certain symptoms or a combination of them may allow the doctor to make a preliminary diagnosis of leukemia. For instance, many leukemia patients share some common problems, such as anemia (low red blood cell count), weakness, bruising easily, and enlarged lymph nodes, liver, and/or spleen.

After collecting information about the patient, including symptoms and family medical background, the doctor needs to perform a routine physical exam.

blood—the red blood cells, white blood cells, and platelets. The test results of a person with leukemia are likely to show a high white blood cell count, and low red blood cell and platelet counts.

The CBC does not require a lot of blood to obtain accurate results. Blood may be collected just by a simple finger stick. Sometimes the blood may be taken from a vein, usually from the arm. The blood sample, collected in a test tube, is mixed with a chemical to keep it from clotting. Then it is sent to a laboratory where it is analyzed by machines. The machines measure the size and number of red blood cells, the amount of hemoglobin present, the number of white blood cells, and the number of platelets.[3] If the results are abnormal, the tests are usually run a second time to confirm the results.[4] Abnormal test results may be a strong indication that leukemia is present, but the CBC test can give only a preliminary diagnosis of leukemia. A complete, accurate diagnosis cannot be made until the bone marrow cells are examined.[5]

Bone Marrow Aspiration

All leukemia patients must undergo a diagnostic bone marrow test. The purpose of this test is to find out what percentage of

A laboratory technician checks the results of a blood test.

the marrow cells are abnormal blasts. Cells are removed in a procedure called a biopsy and analyzed under a microscope to determine the type of leukemia.[6]

During a bone marrow aspiration biopsy, the doctor inserts a long, hollow needle attached to a syringe into the hipbone or the breastbone. Both are large bones that are close to the surface of the body and contain a lot of bone marrow. (The area is numbed with an anesthetic to keep the patient as comfortable as possible.) The needle then sucks up a small amount of fluid containing bone marrow cells; this sample is taken for analysis.

Then the hematologist (a specialist in blood cells and blood-forming tissues) examines the bone marrow sample under a microscope. The cells are stained with dyes so that the structures can be viewed. The specialist can then determine which cells are multiplying uncontrollably and how far they have spread.[7]

The results of a bone marrow test are very important. The findings, which give the specific type of leukemia and the degree of damage, are very helpful in determining an appropriate treatment program.

Spinal Tap (Lumbar Puncture)

Many doctors recommend a spinal tap for their leukemia patients. The purpose of this procedure is to see if the diseased cells have spread to the central nervous system.

To prepare for the spinal tap procedure, the patient must lie down on his or her side and curl up into a ball so that there are spaces between the vertebrae of the spine. The lower spine area is numbed with an anesthetic. The doctor then inserts a small, hollow needle between two vertebrae and allows a sample of cerebrospinal fluid (CSF) to flow out into a syringe. This fluid is then examined under a microscope for the presence of any leukemic cells.[8]

Many patients are afraid of a spinal tap. Medical experts say that this procedure is much less painful if the patient lies still and relaxes—but that is easier said than done. The spinal tap is a very safe procedure, but it can have uncomfortable side effects, including headaches, nausea, vomiting, and difficulty walking (only temporary).[9]

Once diagnostic testing is completed, and the doctor has identified the exact kind of leukemia and has assessed the damage, the treatment process can begin.

5

Treating Leukemia

During his long baseball career with the Minnesota Twins and California Angels, which lasted from 1967 to 1986, Rod Carew broke records—he was a seven-time American League batting champion—and eventually hit his way into the Hall of Fame. Carew later became a batting coach for the Angels and enjoyed a nice, private family life. However, in the fall of 1995, Carew went public about a personal tragedy: His eighteen-year-old daughter, Michelle, had leukemia.

On September 11, 1995, Michelle was writing an English paper when she felt severe pains in her head and neck; her vision was so blurred she could hardly read the words on her computer. Michelle went to the doctor; only four days later, blood tests revealed that she had acute nonlymphocytic leukemia (also known as acute myelogenous leukemia), a rare, aggressive form of the disease.

The doctors told the Carew family that a bone marrow transplant might greatly increase Michelle's chances of survival, but finding a perfect match was unlikely. Neither Michelle's parents nor her two sisters had Michelle's tissue type. Her father, Rod Carew, was of mixed West Indian and Panamanian descent. The chances of finding a suitable match were therefore greatly reduced because minority donors make up a very small percentage of the National Marrow Registry Program. To complicate matters even further, Michelle's mother, Marilyn, had a Russian-Jewish heritage. This mixture dramatically reduced Michelle's odds of finding a perfect bone marrow match, to less than a 10 percent likelihood.

Shortly after Michelle's diagnosis, her health quickly deteriorated. She developed eye problems and almost went blind. Then she almost died when she went into shock because of a bacterial infection. After several rounds of chemotherapy, Michelle's condition improved, and lab tests showed no signs of leukemia. Michelle fought hard to stay well. Unfortunately, within a few weeks she was back in the hospital. Her body had become weakened by the chemotherapy, and she was having trouble fighting off a variety of infections.

On April 17, 1996, Michelle lost her battle with leukemia as she died in the hospital room with her parents by her side.[1] Michelle had a variety of factors working against her: Her leukemia was rare and deadly, and getting a bone marrow transplant was unlikely because of her complex genetic background.

Michelle Carew is comforted by her father, Los Angeles Angels coach Rod Carew, in March 1996. Michelle's complex genetic background made it difficult to find a match from a bone marrow donor.

A few decades ago, the end of Michelle Carew's story would have been typical for leukemia patients, but today's treatments are allowing the majority of young people with leukemia to survive. Back in 1960, even under normal circumstances, the survival rate for children with acute lymphocytic leukemia was only 4 percent. People who developed leukemia usually died within a few months after diagnosis. Today, various new treatments have significantly improved the lifespan as well as the quality of life for leukemia patients. Childhood leukemia is now the most curable form of the disease. As many as 80 percent of children with ALL survive more than five years. Survival rates for the other forms of leukemia have greatly improved as well. The overall survival rate for people with leukemia has risen from 14 percent in 1960 to 42 percent in the late 1990s.[2]

A more typical leukemia story these days is the experience of Lee Grayson, a young New Jersey lawyer. In 1995, when he was thirty-two, he noticed some bruises on his arm and leg. Unlike the usual bumps and bruises he picked up in the course of his active, athletic lifestyle, these didn't fade away. They were still there months later, when a summer cold that hung on sent Grayson to the doctor's office. The doctor was not concerned about the bruises, but Lee asked for a blood test because there were some cases of diabetes in his family, and he was worried that he might be developing the disease, too. He was stunned when he received a call from the doctor a few days later. The test results indicated that Lee might have leukemia, and he had to go in for a biopsy the next day.

The new test results were ominous, and Lee was told that his only chance for survival was a bone marrow transplant. Over the months that followed, Lee's brother, sister, and father were ruled out as possible donors, and experts at the national bone marrow registry searched for a match. A donor was found but backed out two days before Lee was scheduled to fly to Seattle, Washington, for the operation. More months went by, and Lee's condition grew worse. He feared he would not live long enough to find a donor.

Finally, fifteen months after the diagnosis, another match was found. Cheryl Wrigley, a single mother in New Jersey, had attended a bone marrow drive years before and donated a blood sample. When she got the call from the registry, she did not hesitate. After undergoing a number of additional tests, she went to a Philadelphia hospital where bone marrow was drawn from her hip. Meanwhile, Lee Grayson was in the hospital in Seattle being prepared for the transplant. Two days of chemotherapy and four days of powerful radiation treatments wiped out all of his own bone marrow, and then Cheryl's healthy bone marrow cells were transfused into his body. They soon settled down inside Lee's bones, and within a few weeks they were producing normal blood cells.

According to the registry procedures, bone marrow donors and recipients can correspond anonymously for a year, and then can decide whether they wish to meet. Cheryl gave her consent. Since then she and Grayson have met several times, talk on the phone regularly, and exchange cards and gifts. "Without Cheryl, I wouldn't be here," says Lee Grayson. "She was a complete stranger and she saved my life." It was a rewarding experience for Cheryl Wrigley, too. "If I never do another thing in my life," she commented, "I can look in the mirror and say I did something really, really good."[3]

Blood Transfusions

Blood transfusions are often a very effective way to relieve symptoms in leukemia patients. A person with leukemia usually has a very low hematocrit (the volume of red blood cells as a percentage of the total volume of a blood sample). The lack of oxygen-carrying cells often causes anemia, leaving the person weak and tired. In children, a normal hematocrit ranges from 35 to 50 percent. Doctors generally recommend that children receive a red-cell transfusion when the hematocrit falls below 20 percent. The job of blood transfusions is to increase the number of red blood cells and maintain the level of normal red blood cells. Red cell transfusions do very well to keep the blood hemoglobin as normal as possible.

Transfusions are not recommended as a routine way of relieving symptoms, however. Blood transfusions do involve some risks. Although donor blood is carefully screened, there is a small possibility that it might contain viruses causing hepatitis (a 1 in 4,000 risk) or even AIDS (a 1 in 450,000 risk); the recipient might also develop problems due to an imperfect match to all the proteins the donor blood contains. For these reasons, transfusions should be given only in life-threatening situations.

Sometimes platelet transfusions are given to leukemia patients. In leukemia, the platelet numbers are often so low that the patient could bleed to death from a minor cut. In children, a platelet count normally reads from between 150,000/mm^3 to 420,000/mm^3. The platelet count often drops sharply during chemotherapy treatments. Children whose platelet count goes below 10,000 to 20,000/mm^3 are usually given platelet transfusions.

Platelet transfusions also involve some possible dangers.

Like red cell transfusions, platelet transfusions pose a small risk of infection by hepatitis or HIV viruses. Therefore, platelet transfusions should also be considered only when they are absolutely necessary.[4]

Chemotherapy

Chemotherapy is the most effective approach in fighting leukemia. The word *chemotherapy* means treatment with chemicals. The chemicals used in leukemia treatment are powerful drugs designed to destroy abnormal white blood cells or interfere with their development. The main objective of chemotherapy is to achieve remission. In remission, there are no longer any symptoms of the disease. During remission, laboratory tests of blood and bone marrow samples show no abnormal white blood cells. That does not mean that the disease is cured, however. Leukemic blasts may still be present in small numbers somewhere in the body, and they may return to the bone marrow or blood later. The return of a patient's cancer is called a relapse. However, people can stay in remission for months or many years. A relapse is most likely to occur within five years after treatment is completed. After five years, relapse is unlikely, and the disease is considered "cured."

How does chemotherapy work? Most of the drugs effective against cancers work at the stage when the cancerous cells are reproducing, dividing to make copies of themselves. Because cancer cells typically divide much more actively than normal cells, they tend to soak up most of the poisonous drugs. Unfortunately, some normal cells that divide fairly often are also killed by the drugs. As a result, healthy cells in the bone marrow, hair, skin, and the lining of the mouth and digestive system may be damaged.[5] This causes side effects such as hair loss, nausea and vomiting, mouth sores, headache, and loss of appetite. The side effects are usually not life-threatening and go away after the treatment is completed.

Chemotherapy generally involves a three-step process with variations, depending on the type of leukemia. Following is the treatment series for ALL, the most common type of leukemia found in children.

Two young girls with acute lymphocytic leukemia (ALL) play while they receive chemotherapy treatment. Hair loss is a common side effect of chemotherapy. The strong drugs used to kill the cancer can affect the healthy cells of the skin and hair. Luckily, these side effects are not life-threatening and go away after the drug treatments are completed.

Induction therapy. In this first stage of chemotherapy, large doses of anticancer drugs are used to kill as many leukemic cells as quickly as possible until the person goes into remission. This is the most intensive stage of treatment. Induction therapy may take up to four weeks or as long as twelve weeks.

Consolidation therapy. This second stage takes place once the patient is in remission. Even though there are no signs of leukemia during remission, there may still be cancer cells hiding out somewhere in the body. Now a new combination of drugs is used to kill any remaining cancer cells that may have escaped the attack during the induction stage.

Maintenance therapy. In this final stage, the patient must take ongoing low-dose anticancer drugs for two to three years. The purpose is to kill any remaining leukemic cells and keep the disease from returning. This is a very important step. If treatment is stopped too soon, the disease may come back. Fortunately, this stage of treatment is not as hard on the patient as the induction and consolidation stages.[6]

More than fifty different drugs are now available for chemotherapy.[7] In leukemia, effective treatment depends on the type of leukemia, the severity of the disease, and the person being treated. A drug treatment that works well for one leukemia patient may not work for another. Chemotherapy drugs may be used singly but are used mostly in combination because this strategy increases the chances of killing the cells. Different drugs work on cells in different ways. One kind of drug may act on cells in one stage of development while another drug aims at a different stage.

The various chemotherapy drugs are classified in six main groups:[8]

Alkylating agents are drugs that kill cancer cells by interfering with DNA and RNA, both of which contain the cells' genetic information. This, in turn, prevents the cells from dividing. An alkylating agent commonly used in chemotherapy is cyclophosphamide.

Antimetabolites are drugs that replace important cell nutrients such as folic acid with similar (but not useful) substances. The cancer cells starve to death. (Patients treated with this kind of drug should not take extra folic acid or the treatment will not be as effective.) Some antimetabolites commonly used in chemotherapy are methotrexate, mercaptopurine, and cytarabine. Hydroxyurea is also classified as an antimetabolite. It is a very simple chemical, but scientists are not sure exactly how it works. Hydroxyurea is very effective in fighting leukemic cells. It is also used in treatments of various other cancers, as well as AIDS and sickle cell anemia.

Antibiotic-derivatives are drugs that block the reproduction of cancer cells. Some antibiotics used in chemotherapy are doxorubicin and daunorubicin.

Alkaloids are drugs derived from plants that interrupt cell division, stopping the reproduction of cancer cells. Some alkaloids used in chemotherapy are vincristine and vinblastine, which are derived from the periwinkle plant.

Hormones are chemicals that control and coordinate cell activities. The hormone drugs used in leukemia act to slow cell growth. Some hormone drugs used in chemotherapy are prednisone and dexamethasone. They are both steroids.

Enzymes are proteins that affect chemical reactions. An enzyme drug used in chemotherapy is asparaginase, which breaks down a key amino acid (one of the building blocks for proteins) and thus keeps cancer cells from reproducing by stopping their production of protein.

All chemotherapy drugs have their risks. It is important to speak to the doctor beforehand about possible side effects, and to report any problems associated with the drug.

Keep an Eye on the Blood Counts!

Throughout treatment, patients must have periodic blood tests. The poisonous drugs in the bloodstream can destroy normal blood cells, and it is important to keep an eye on the blood counts. When the number of normal white blood cells is too low, the body becomes defenseless against illnesses. A simple cold can turn deadly.

The blood tests used are a CBC test and a differential. The CBC test includes the total white cell count; the differential gives a list of each type of white blood cell and its percentage of the total. Neutrophils make up the majority of the white blood cells. When their numbers drop, there could be trouble. The absolute neutrophil count (ANC), calculated from the differential, is also important. A child whose ANC is over 1,000 has enough neutrophils to protect the body from illnesses. However, if the ANC falls below 1,000, the patient should be exposed only to healthy people. If the number falls below 200, the patient should be quarantined, or isolated from other people.[9]

Radiation Therapy

Radiation therapy, also called radiotherapy, is used only in high-risk leukemia cases. Radiation therapy involves the use of high doses of X rays to kill cancer cells deep inside the body. A special machine is used to direct an X-ray beam to the area of the body that needs treatment. Cancer cells are destroyed because the X rays impair those cells' ability to divide. As in chemotherapy, some normal cells are also killed in radiation therapy. But in radiotherapy, the destruction of normal cells is minimized because the healthy areas are shielded from the radiation exposure. The treatment is usually given every day for more than two weeks.

Unlike Marie Curie's experience, radiation therapy will not make patients radioactive. It does, however, have some possible dangers. Some people experience mild burns, scarring, nausea, vomiting, weight loss, and hair loss. Symptoms usually go away within a month or two after treatment. There may be a longer-term danger, however: Ironically, radiation therapy may cause cancer.

Radiation therapy is used primarily for people whose cancer has spread to the central nervous system and for people who are receiving bone marrow transplants.[10]

Bone Marrow Transplants

Bone marrow transplantation (BMT) is another method of treatment for leukemia patients. This form of treatment has given hope to thousands of people with leukemia, a disease

61

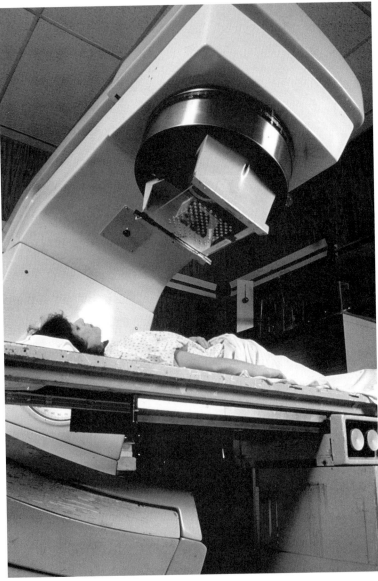

Radiation therapy uses high doses of X rays to kill cancer cells deep inside the body. A special machine directs the beam of X rays to the part of the body that needs treatment.

that was once considered incurable. Patients who cannot be cured by chemotherapy and/or radiation therapy are good candidates for bone marrow transplants. BMT should be considered only for people with certain types of leukemia: chronic myelogenous leukemia, acute myelogenous leukemia, or relapsed acute lymphocytic leukemia.

In a bone marrow transplant, the patient's diseased bone marrow is destroyed with high doses of chemotherapy and/or radiation therapy. It is then replaced with healthy bone marrow. The transplant is not a surgical procedure. The BMT is done in the patient's hospital room. The patient receives the marrow through a needle, just like a blood transfusion. The new marrow is carried by the bloodstream to the cavities of the large bones, where it settles down and begins to produce healthy new blood cells.[11]

To ensure success in BMT, the leukemia patient must be genetically compatible with the bone marrow donor. Everybody has special proteins called human leukocyte-associated antigens (HLA) on the surface of white blood cells in the bone marrow. The HLA antigens can distinguish their own body cells from those of another person's. They are part of the body's immune defenses against germs and foreign chemicals, acting as signals that call white blood cells to attack the invader. Scientists have identified six different HLA antigens that determine the HLA type. If there is not an exact match between the HLA antigens of the donor and the recipient, a serious reaction may develop. In most tissue and organ transplants, mismatched antigens can activate the recipient's immune defenses and result in destruction (rejection) of the transplant. In the case of bone marrow transplants, more often the white blood cells that are alerted to a mismatch of HLA antigens are those from the donor, and they attack the patient's body tissues and organs. This kind of reaction, called graft-versus-host disease (GVHD), occurs in 30 to 50 percent of people who have undergone a transplant where the donor was unrelated or mismatched. It can produce symptoms ranging from a mild skin rash to severe damage to the liver, stomach, or intestines. Steroid hormones and drugs such as cyclosporin and methotrexate may be used to prevent and treat GVHD.[12]

HLA genes are inherited. The best chances of finding a bone marrow donor come from a close relative. Identical twins are 100 percent compatible. Siblings have a 35 percent chance of being a match.[13] Parents, however, are rarely a perfect match. The chances of getting a bone marrow match from an unrelated donor used to be very unlikely. These days, however, many suitable matches can be found due to the growing number of people being listed in various national and international marrow registries.

Although bone marrow transplants are often life-saving, they do involve risks and can cause serious complications. The patient is very susceptible to illnesses after the transplant. The immune system takes time to get back to normal. It may take anywhere from six months to one year to recover completely. In the meantime, the patient should avoid exposure to people with illnesses, even a simple cold.

There are three different types of bone marrow transplants:

At the hospital, Sadako's best friend, Chizuko, told her about an old Japanese legend that says if a person folds one thousand paper cranes, then the gods will grant a wish. Sadako tried very hard to fold as many paper cranes as she could, hoping that the gods would grant her wish: to be healthy enough to run again. Unfortunately, she was able to finish only 644 cranes before she died at the age of twelve. Sadako had a profound effect on her friends and classmates. She was admired for her courage and determination. The remaining 356 paper cranes were completed by her classmates and buried with her. School children all over Japan raised money to build a statue to honor Sadako and all the other children affected by the bomb.

In 1958, a statue of Sadako holding a golden crane was completed and set up in Hiroshima Peace Park. Every year, children from all over the world fold paper cranes and send them to Hiroshima where they are placed around the statue. Sadako's paper crane has become a symbol of peace throughout the world.[1]

Sadako's story is a reminder of the devastating dangers of radiation. Although there is no immediate danger of nuclear weapons being used in war, there is currently an ongoing controversy about nuclear testing and the effects it has on the environment.

We are exposed to radiation every day. Nuclear reactors are used as an alternative supply of energy; radiation is also widely used in medicine in both diagnosis and treatment. In the past, people were often exposed to radiation, but were unaware of the possible dangers. Even the Curie family, who constantly worked with radioactive substances, did not realize they should have taken precautions. Today, we are well aware of the dangers. In work with radiation, preventive measures have become standard practice.

The Dangers of Nuclear Testing

Sadako's story has touched people all over the world. She has been an important inspiration in the peace movement. The major world powers continue to work hard for peace. Nuclear weapons have never again been used in warfare; however, many countries still continue to develop them. At first, nuclear weapons were tested by exploding them in the atmosphere, but there was a growing concern about what the effects of the tests were doing to the environment. Activists were determined to stop nuclear testing.

On September 10, 1996, the United Nations General Assembly voted to approve a Nuclear Test Ban Treaty. However, some smaller countries have refused to comply with the treaty and have continued to test bombs in the air. The treaty has other problems, too. Some world powers, including the United States, conduct "subcritical" testing, which involves nuclear explosions hundreds of feet below ground. "Subcritical" testing is not included in the Nuclear Test Ban Treaty, but underground nuclear testing is still controversial.[2] Is it safe? What kind of effect will it have on the environment? Will radiation somehow escape into the atmosphere? What will it do to the water?

This woman and her daughter visit the Sadako memorial in Hiroshima Peace Park in Japan. Every year, thousands of children from all over the world fold paper cranes and send them to honor Sadako's memory (see the piles of paper cranes, lower right). On top of the memorial is a statue of Sadako holding her crane.

We have seen what radiation can do to the environment and to people who are exposed to it. To protect the communities and the lives of countless people, efforts to eliminate nuclear testing around the world will continue.

Nuclear Power Plants

Nuclear energy does not have to be harmful. Scientists have developed ways to use nuclear energy as a safe source of power that provides us with electricity. Nuclear power plants have been established all over the world to generate the world's electricity. At the end of 1993, there were 430 nuclear power plants worldwide. The United States has the largest nuclear energy program in the world, with more than one hundred nuclear power plants.

How safe are nuclear power plants? That question has been an ongoing controversy since 1979, when an accident at a nuclear power plant at Three Mile Island in Middletown, Pennsylvania, created a scare. Fortunately, only a small amount of radiation was released and had no effect on the environment. But the incident forced people to think about what kind of devastation it could have caused.

In April 1986, the unthinkable did happen. A horrendous accident occurred at the Chernobyl nuclear power plant in Ukraine. A nuclear reactor, running with its safety features turned off, melted down, spewing dangerous radioactive materials over not only the local area but surrounding countries as well. Whole communities in the area around Chernobyl were destroyed, and 130,000 people had to leave their homes because it was no longer safe to live there or grow crops on the contaminated soil. In addition to those injured and killed directly in the accident, radiation caused a noticeable increase in cases of thyroid cancer over the next decade, and scientists suspected that the leukemia rate might also increase.[3]

Nevertheless, most nuclear power plants have been extremely safe. However, even if there is never another deadly accident, there is another important concern: Nuclear power plants produce radioactive wastes. These have been piling up over the years, while researchers have been looking for safe ways to dispose of them. Ideas have ranged from burying the waste products in deep, stable underground caverns to calcination (burning them so that only a dry powder remains), or combining them with cement to form solid concrete blocks. The most promising way appears to be vitrification, or sealing the wastes into a solid glass compound that will be stable for thousands of years. Still, there is no agreement on where to put the wastes.[4]

Radiation in Medicine

In medicine, radiation is widely used to study, diagnose, and treat patients. The patient's body is directly exposed to the radiation. Doctors use X rays to display images of the patient's bones and organs. Dentists X-ray teeth to locate cavities.

Unlike in the days of the Curie family, however, strict precautions are now taken for all medical procedures and testing. These days, the exposure to radiation in medicine is minimal. Radiation is used in very low doses, not enough to do any harm, but many tests involving radiation might still cause damages that accumulate in a person's body and could possibly cause leukemia or some other illness sometime in the future. However, doctors are now well aware of the risks and order tests only when they are necessary.

Both patients and medical personnel are carefully protected during X-ray testing. It is standard practice for the patient to wear a lead apron to protect the vital organs from the radiation. Technicians and doctors usually leave the room while the X-ray picture is being taken because they are exposed to the radiation on a daily basis. If they stayed in the room, the continual exposure to radiation, even at such low levels, would put them at a much greater risk than the patient, who is exposed only once or twice a year.

X Rays in Shoe Stores?

Many years ago, before scientists realized the dangers of radiation, some shoe stores used special X-ray machines called fluoroscopes to "diagnose" a person's foot. The fluoroscope showed an image of the foot's bone structure and the outside part of the shoe. This helped the salesperson to see if the new shoe provided enough room around the toes and to figure out the customer's correct shoe size. When more was learned about the dangers of radiation, fluoroscopes were removed from the shoe stores. They are still used for medical purposes, however. As in other X-ray testing, careful precautions are taken.

Radiation treatments have greatly improved over the years. Years ago, the radiation dose to treat cancer was much higher than it is now. This often caused more harm than good. Scientists have discovered how to lower the doses and make the treatments much more effective. Radiation treatments have saved thousands of lives.

Toxic Waste Hazards

In Woburn, Massachusetts, just outside of Boston, a cluster of leukemia cases were linked to toxic wastes that had seeped into the town's drinking water. Between 1969 and 1979, there were nineteen cases of leukemia in Woburn—four times the national leukemia rate.[5] This story has been publicized in a best-selling book and movie (1999) called *A Civil Action*.

For years, residents in Woburn got their water from six wells (called A through F). But in the 1950s, there was a water shortage, and the city officials wanted to drill two more wells in another part of town. Some officials warned that this water was of poor quality, but the wells were drilled anyway—well G in 1964, and well H in 1968. Residents noticed that the water from these two wells smelled and tasted really bad. The water also ate holes in the plumbing. Local and state health officials repeatedly tested the water, but according to their results, the water was just unpleasant, not unsafe.

During the 1970s, however, an increasing number of children in Woburn were developing leukemia and other illnesses. One parent, Anne Anderson, whose child was dying of leukemia, felt strongly that the water was causing her son's illness. No one would listen to her concerns; people thought she was crazy.

Finally, in 1979, Anne Anderson was proven right. There was a toxic waste dump nearby, and town officials discovered some barrels that had been dumped just several thousand feet from the wells. The wells were tested for the presence of the chemicals contained in the barrels and found to have very high toxic readings. The water had been contaminated with some highly poisonous, cancer-causing chemicals. Chemicals from the toxic waste dump had seeped into the ground and from there into the community's water system. Both wells were closed immediately.

During the 1980s, eight families from Woburn filed a lawsuit against two major corporations, Beatrice Foods and a manufacturing company, W. R. Grace. These companies were accused of dumping chemicals that eventually led to the death of several children from leukemia. The lawsuit turned into an eight-year-long legal battle, which turned out not to have a very satisfactory ending for the families involved. Ultimately, the case against Beatrice was dismissed. In the case of W. R. Grace, a guilty verdict was thrown out of court because of confusion concerning a time frame. Finally, the families settled out of court with the companies they were suing and were awarded several million dollars each. But neither company ever admitted to being responsible for the deaths of the children in Woburn.[6]

Back in the early 1970s, people were unwilling to believe that such a destructive contamination could occur. The

Environmental Protection Agency (EPA) and other major environmental organizations did not exist as they do today. In the seventies, Anne Anderson could not find anyone who was willing to test the brown, foul-smelling water that was coming from her faucets.

Today, we live in an environmentally conscious world. People have created organizations to protect the environment, which in turn, protects the people. Toxic dumps must be cleaned up, and water regulations are very strict. These measures are helping to prevent leukemia by reducing people's exposure to carcinogens in the environment.

On September 28, 1986, Donna Robbins, Anne Anderson, and Patrick Toomey, plaintiffs in the Woburn case, discuss the settlement that was reached the day before with the W. R. Grace company.

7

Leukemia and Society

In March 1988, Anissa Ayala had just turned sixteen when she was diagnosed with chronic myelogenous leukemia, an adult form of the disease. In cases like Anissa's, the patient is likely to die within five years after diagnosis. Only one thing could save Anissa's life—a bone marrow transplant. Since siblings have the best chance of being a perfect match, Anissa's brother, Airon, was tested. But he was not a match. Anissa's parents, Mary and Abe, were also tested, as were other close relatives. All the test results came back negative. Then Anissa's family began a nationwide search for bone marrow donors. They even went public to ask for people to get tested. But time was running out, and the Ayalas still could not find a compatible bone marrow donor for Anissa.

Desperate to save their daughter's life, Mary and Abe Ayala made an important decision: They would have another baby in hopes that this new baby's tissue type would match Anissa's. There were a lot of odds against them. Abe had had a vasectomy, a surgical procedure to make him sterile, many years before. Although vasectomies can sometimes be reversed, Abe had only a 50 percent chance of fathering a child. Mary's chances of getting pregnant were also lower than normal because she was forty-one years old at the time. Moreover, even if Mary did get pregnant, there was only a 25 percent chance that the new baby would share the same tissue type as Anissa. Another drawback was that even if the new sibling did turn out to be a perfect match, Anissa still only had a 40 percent chance of surviving five years after the transplant.

In July 1989, Mary beat the odds and became pregnant. The Ayalas had already decided that they wanted this baby no matter what happened, even if there was not a bone marrow match. At four months of the pregnancy, Mary and Abe found out through medical tests that their baby was a healthy girl. When Mary was seven months pregnant, tests revealed that the baby, whom they already called Marissa, was a perfect match! On April 3, 1990, Marissa Eve Ayala was born.

On May 22, 1991, Marissa, now fourteen months old, was ready for the long-awaited procedure. On June 4, 1991, the bone marrow transplant took place. Before removing some of her bone marrow, baby Marissa was given general anesthesia. The doctor assured her parents that the risks to Marissa were minimal; she would just have a little soreness in the hip area. When little Marissa woke up, she was smiling at her parents as she always did after waking up from a nap. Marissa was ready to go home from the hospital later that day.

Meanwhile, Anissa had received chemotherapy and radiation treatments to destroy her own bone marrow, and then Marissa's marrow cells were infused into her body. A few weeks after the bone marrow transplant, Anissa's condition had greatly improved. One year later, she married her boyfriend, Bryan Espinosa, who had stuck by her throughout her difficult battle. Anissa hopes to have children someday, even though her doctor has warned her that the chemotherapy and

On her wedding day bride Anissa Ayala holds her little sister, Marissa, who donated bone marrow that saved Anissa's life. To the right, is their mother, Mary, who conceived the child specifically to try to save her older daughter's life.

radiation treatments she has undergone may make it unlikely that she can conceive. She is now well past the five-year remission period after which cancer patients are considered cured.[1]

Ethical Dilemmas

The Ayala story sparked a great deal of controversy about ethics in modern medicine. How much control does (and should) a person have over his or her own body? Does a person have a right to donate an organ? In most cases, the answer is yes. In the Ayala case, the question arose: Does a parent have the right to donate a child's organ when the child cannot give an informed consent? And is it ethical to conceive a baby specially for the purpose of providing a transplant to another child whose life is threatened?

The Ayalas received many letters and even threatening phone calls from people criticizing their actions. Some critics actually accused the Ayalas of having a baby to serve as body parts. For the Ayalas, however, that was not the case. They never considered aborting the child, no matter what the test results showed. They were committed to having their baby, to loving and nurturing it, whether or not it would provide a match for Anissa.[2]

One supporter pointed out that among all the reasons to have a baby, theirs was a good one. People have babies for many different reasons: to work on the family farm, or other family businesses; to take care of parents in their old age; to produce an heir; to provide siblings to another child; and to have an extension of a person's ego.[3]

In fact, doctors admit that many people have conceived children to provide donor tissue for a relative, but the Ayalas were the first to go public with their decision.[4] According to a survey taken at bone marrow centers in 1991, forty families admitted to their doctor that they had conceived a baby for the purpose of producing an organ donor.[5]

A 1991 issue of *Time* magazine reported on a survey that asked, "Is it morally acceptable for parents to conceive a child in order to obtain an organ or tissue to save the life of another of their children?" The results: 47 percent answered "yes," and 37 percent answered "no."[6]

Other ethical questions were also raised about organ transplants. Can somebody force another person to donate an organ or even to be tested? In Illinois, twelve-year-old Jean-Pierre Bosze, who was diagnosed with leukemia in 1988, could not find a compatible bone marrow donor. In 1990, Jean-Pierre's father, Tamas, filed a lawsuit against Nancy Curran, a woman he had had an affair with four years earlier. As a result of this affair, Nancy had given birth to twins. Tamas knew that Jean-Pierre's half brother and half sister had a good chance of being a bone marrow match. Tamas took Nancy to court, trying to force her to have her twins' blood tested, and if there were a match, to make them donate bone marrow to their sick half brother.

Ultimately, the Illinois judge in charge of the case ruled that although there is minimal risk to the donor, or in this case donors, the twins could not be forced to donate their marrow or to be tested because either action would be an invasion of their right to privacy.[7]

The Search for Bone Marrow Donors

Every year, thousands of leukemia patients die because they cannot find suitable bone marrow donors. Only a small percentage of the donors listed in the national marrow donor registry are members of minority groups. Over the last decade, efforts to publicize the desperate need for minority donors have led to a significant increase in numbers in the national marrow donor registry.

JoAnne Johnson, whose story was told in Chapter 4, was the inspiration for one of the first crusades to publicize the need for minority bone marrow donors. JoAnne was African-American, and in early 1989, when she desperately needed a compatible donor, there were only eight hundred black donors listed in the transplant registry. JoAnne and her family dedicated their lives to publicizing their plight and the need for donors. Unfortunately, it was too late to save JoAnne, but her family continued their work even after JoAnne's death in February 1990. Their efforts helped many African-American leukemia patients in need of bone marrow transplants. Within six months after JoAnne's death, the Johnson family and the volunteers who responded to their pleas had extended the eight hundred black donors in 1989 into a list of about sixteen thousand donors.[8]

When ten-year-old Katrina Whetstone was diagnosed with leukemia in 1988, there were only a few hundred black donors

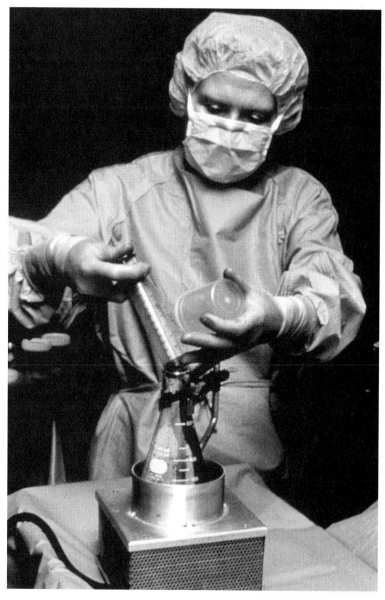

The hospital technician is transferring bone marrow collected from a donor into a bag that will store the marrow safely.

in the national registry. Thanks to the Johnson family's efforts, there were thousands when Katrina was seeking a bone marrow donor. In August 1991, Katrina found a bone marrow donor—a thirty-six-year-old African-American woman. Fortunately, Katrina's bone marrow transplant was a success.[9]

In 1995, there was still a major need for black bone marrow donors. Only 5 percent of the 1.8 million donors in the National Marrow Donor Program at that time were African Americans. The Carew family also started a big campaign to publicize the need for bone marrow donors. Michelle had convinced her usually private father to speak to the public about her plight. She told him, "Daddy, you've got to let people know about this. Not just for me, for all the kids who need transplants." Rod Carew enlisted some old friends from baseball to help him publicize his daughter's condition and the desperate need for bone marrow donors, especially minorities. Because of the Carew family's efforts, more than seventy thousand calls were made to the hotline of the National Marrow Donor Program in Minneapolis, and the number of African-American donors listed in the bone marrow registry was greatly expanded.[10]

Coping with Leukemia

Like many other diseases, leukemia has a serious impact on the patient's life. The leukemia patient must deal with both physical and emotional challenges. Leukemia stirs up a lot of emotional feelings for both patients and their families. They may become frightened, angry, sad, upset, and confused.

People often feel hopeless and helpless because they think that leukemia is a "deadly disease." Many people are not aware of the encouraging developments in recently approved leukemia treatments. Education is a very important tool for coping with leukemia. The more people learn about this disease, the more they will understand it and realize that a leukemia diagnosis is not an automatic death sentence. Knowledge can be very comforting.

Leukemia patients find that the life they once knew has suddenly changed after diagnosis. It is very hard for parents to watch their children battling such a debilitating illness. It can be a very traumatic time for all loved ones—parents, siblings, relatives, friends, and classmates.

School is often a major concern for young patients. They wonder, will I ever go back? What will my classmates think about me? Will people understand?

Many children do not understand the disease. Some worry that they will catch it from someone else who has leukemia. This can put a real emotional strain on the leukemia patient. Teachers should be told about the child's situation and should then inform the students, to eliminate any confusion. Patients are able to cope much better when they have a good support system, with friends who understand.

Leukemia can be a real test for relationships. Anissa Ayala's boyfriend helped her through her battle and stuck by her no matter what. However, not all relationships can withstand the physical and emotional stresses involved in battling a disease. Leukemia patients also worry about whether or not they can

Some people worry that they can catch leukemia from someone who has it. This is not true. Patients can cope much better if they have friends who understand.

conceive children. Anissa had to face this problem. Chemotherapy and radiation treatments can impair a person's ability to have children by damaging their reproductive cells (eggs or sperm). Again, education can help leukemia patients and the people close to them understand the problems and the possibilities for solving them.

8

Leukemia and the Future

When Rachel Smith was born late in 1997 at Holyoke Hospital in Massachusetts, her doctors did something different from the usual birth procedure. The placenta (the special organ that nourishes a developing baby inside its mother's womb) is normally thrown away after it passes out of the mother's body. But when the doctors cut Rachel's umbilical cord, they did not throw away the placenta still attached to it. Instead, they carefully drained blood (referred to as "cord blood") out of both the placenta and the umbilical cord and stored that blood in a freezer at the University of Massachusetts Medical Center in Worcester. Not long afterward, the American Cord Blood Program at the medical center was notified that one of the batches of cord blood stored there had found a match: a five-year-old

Australian boy who had leukemia and needed a transplant. Because the program keeps records confidential, Rachel's family will never be sure that her cord blood was the batch sent to help the boy in Australia. Still, Rachel's mother likes to think of her as an infant medical heroine.[1]

Umbilical Cord Blood for Transplants

Doctors are now able to treat many leukemia patients with something that used to be thrown away. The blood in the placenta and umbilical cord is rich in stem cells, the primitive cells that develop into red blood cells, white blood cells, and platelets. Cord blood transplants can be used for leukemia patients who cannot find a suitable bone marrow donor or are too sick to wait until a donor is found.

In 1998, *The New England Journal of Medicine* reported on the largest study of cord blood transplants conducted so far. The study involved 562 patients, more than 400 of whom were children. These patients were very ill and could not find compatible donors for a bone marrow transplant. Without a transplant, they would probably die, so they were given cord blood instead. By 100 days after the transplant, 218 of the 562 patients had died. This rate was similar to the survival rate seen in bone marrow transplants from nonrelated donors.[2]

Dr. Joanne Kurtzberg of Duke University Medical Center, where 170 of the study's 562 transplants were performed, commented, "I do think that this may ultimately replace unrelated bone marrow (transplants), but we're 10 years away from that."[3] Dr. Kurtzberg's opinion is based on the fact that cord blood transplants have more benefits and fewer risks than bone marrow transplants.

In cord blood transplants, the donor is not harmed in any way. Blood is taken from the umbilical cord and placenta right after birth. (The stem cells would be gone within twenty-four hours.) The blood is then frozen and stored until it is needed. Doctors call the stem cells in cord blood "naive," because the immune system of a newborn baby is not fully developed yet, and the cells have not been sensitized to "foreign" antigens. Patients who receive cord blood transplants are thus much less likely to develop graft-versus-host disease (GVHD). Cord blood does not have to match the recipient's tissue type as closely as it does with bone marrow transplants. With cord blood, there can be successful treatments with only three, four, or five matching antigens. (The more matches, though, the better the chances of success.) Cord blood is also less likely than bone marrow to transmit infections from a donor who had been exposed to a variety of disease-causing germs. Another benefit is that the young stem cells have an enormous potential for growth and multiply quickly in the recipient's bone marrow. In addition, only a few ounces of cord blood are needed for the transplant, whereas as much as a quart or more is needed for bone marrow transplants.[4]

Another advantage of cord blood transplants is that they are less costly than bone marrow transplants. In 1998, cord blood for a transplant, obtained from a public bank like the one at the University of Massachusetts, cost about $15,000, which in most cases would be covered by the patient's health insurance. A matched bone marrow specimen would cost from $20,000 to $30,000. That figure does not count the up to $10,000 spent in searching for a match, a process that is not covered by insurance.[5]

In addition to public cord banks, private companies are now storing cord blood for the families who donated it, just in case a family member might need a transplant later. These companies charge $1,000 to $1,500, plus a small annual fee.[6] Except for families who already have a child with leukemia or lymphoma, the odds of using stored cord blood are estimated at about one in one hundred thousand.[7] That seems like a rather remote chance, but one private California company

Banking on Cord Blood

The New York Blood Center in Manhattan started the first, and now the largest, public cord blood bank in the world. They provided the cord blood that was used in the large-scale study reported in 1998. The Blood Center has a supply of almost nine thousand units of cord blood. Each week, the New York center needs to find a donor for the twenty to thirty patients around the world who ask for help. About 60 percent of these people are able to find a suitable match. If cord blood is to replace bone marrow in most transplants, however, a lot more of it will be needed. It is estimated that about one hundred thousand units of cord blood would be required to provide matches for 85 to 95 percent of patients all over the world who need transplants.[8]

banked more than ten thousand specimens in three years—more than the largest public bank collected in six years.[9]

Many scientists find the prospects of cord blood transplants very exciting. Cord blood can be used to help thousands of people who cannot find a compatible bone marrow donor and do not have the time to wait. This would be especially beneficial to African Americans and other minority groups.[10] Cord blood may even be used to treat other diseases, such as sickle cell anemia and AIDS.

Dr. Claude Lenfant, director of the National Heart, Lung, and Blood Institute, which financed the cord blood study, found the prospects of cord blood transplants "fantastic," but he remained cautiously optimistic. Dr. Lenfant added that cord blood transplants are still a very new treatment that needs to be studied further.[11]

Matchmaking Made Easier

In October 1998, an article published in *The New England Journal of Medicine* reported a new technique that may give thousands of additional people a chance to receive a potentially life-saving bone marrow transplant. This new technique makes it possible for bone marrow transplants to be performed successfully with "mismatched," related donors.

Researchers at Israel's Weizmann Institute of Science and Italy's Perugia University studied forty-three people with leukemia who could not be cured by chemotherapy and/or radiation therapy. In the study, stem cells were taken from donors and were treated with high doses of drugs and/or radiation to get rid of the T cells, the white blood cells that attack foreign cells. This process eliminates the danger of a graft-versus-host reaction, even if there is not a perfect match between donor and recipient. The immune cells in the transplant that could attack the patient's body have been removed. With this method, only three HLA antigens need to match. The researchers found that twelve of the forty-three patients in the study had no signs of leukemia eighteen months after receiving a transplant of treated marrow stem cells. The success rate was similar to that in people receiving transplants from matched, unrelated donors.[12]

The results of the study were especially impressive, considering that these leukemia patients would have died without the transplant. This technique also makes it possible to treat people with acute forms of leukemia, who do not have time to wait. Finding an exact match might take a longer time than they can afford.[13]

Another new approach was developed at the Dana-Farber Cancer Institute in Boston. Before the transplant, the donor's marrow is exposed for thirty-six hours to cells from the recipient, together with a protein called CTLA-4-Ig. This protein binds to the recipient's cells and prevents them from stimulating an attack by T cells in the donor's marrow. The number of T cells capable of recognizing the recipient's cells as "foreign" is greatly reduced, and therefore the development of a graft-versus-host reaction is greatly reduced, even if the donor and recipient are not well matched. In a study reported in June 1999, twelve patients with leukemia or inherited

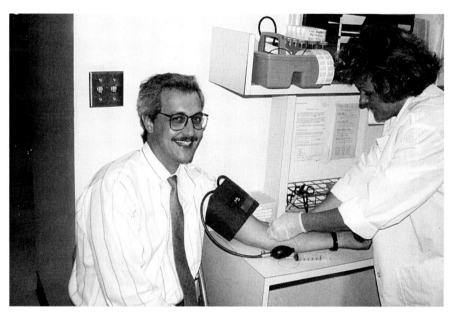

This man has volunteered to donate bone marrow for transplants. Here he is having his blood pressure tested as part of an overall physical examination to determine whether he will be a good candidate to donate marrow.

blood diseases were given transplants of treated bone marrow from "mismatched" donors, only half of whose HLA antigens matched those of the recipients. None of the patients in the study developed severe GVHD, although normally, 70 to 90 percent of them would have been expected to have a severe reaction. Moreover, the new technique has another advantage. Patients who receive transplants of untreated bone marrow must take antirejection drugs for the rest of their lives. These drugs knock out all the T cells and leave the patients vulnerable to infection by viruses and bacteria and at high risk of later developing cancer. On the other hand, those who

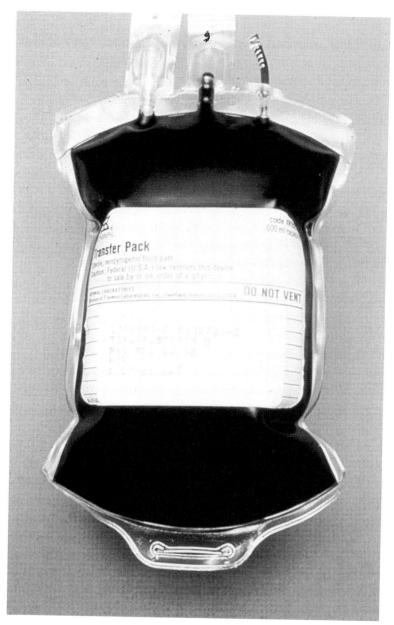

A bone marrow bag, containing precious material for transplants.

receive marrow treated to make it "tolerant" of their antigens will not need to take antirejection drugs because only the T cells responsible for rejection have been inactivated. The T cells that defend the body against infections and cancer are still intact and able to fight other diseases.[14]

Better Targeting for Drugs

Doctors and researchers involved with chemotherapy have long dreamed of finding "magic bullets," or drugs that can wipe out just their target (whether it is a disease germ or a cancerous cell) without harming normal cells. However, since cancer cells share most of the same genetic information and chemical makeup as the normal cells in the body, the drugs that kill the cancer cells or stop their growth usually do the same thing to some "good" cells in the body.

Recently, advances in genetics and other basic science have allowed researchers to learn more about the nature and reactions of living cells. They have been using the knowledge they gain to seek more effective ways of stopping harmful processes and helping normal cells to defend themselves.

Even with knowledge, the search for new treatments can be long and laborious. Back in the 1960s, for example, Dr. Judah Folkman, a cancer researcher at Children's Hospital in Boston, discovered that cancerous tumors need a rich blood supply to continue their uncontrolled growth. Folkman found that tumors actually produce a hormonelike chemical that stimulates surrounding tissues to form new blood vessels to help feed the tumor's growth. For many years, he searched for ways to combat this chemical, and to cut off the tumor's blood supply. Finally, in the late 1980s, Dr. Folkman and his colleagues found some drugs that could stop angiogenesis, the formation of new blood vessels. Preliminary results in human cancer patients showed that these drugs slowed the growth of their tumors. But more effective drugs were still needed.

Over the next decade, Dr. Folkman and one of his post-doctoral students, Dr. Michael O'Reilly, working with chemists, discovered and isolated two substances that stopped angiogenesis. Ironically, one was produced by cancerous tumors themselves. It worked to keep new tumors from growing and competing with the main tumor for the body's resources. This substance, which Dr. Folkman named angiostatin, was present in the urine of mice with cancerous tumors, but in such tiny amounts that Dr. O'Reilly had to collect 10 quarts (9.5 liters) of mouse urine to isolate 0.03 ounce (0.85 gram) of angiostatin. The other drug, named endostatin, is produced by the lining of blood vessels; it is a fragment of a very common protein, collagen, found in many body structures.

In experiments on mice, both angiostatin and endostatin were effective against various kinds of solid tumors, and when they were used together, the tumors not only stopped growing, but shrank until they disappeared and did not return. The mice were cured. Surprisingly, these anticancer drugs also worked against leukemia, even though this blood cancer is not usually regarded as a solid tumor. Dr. Folkman found that for leukemia to develop, new blood vessels must be formed in the bone marrow. Then leukemia tumors grow along these blood vessels "like berries on a bush" and shed cancerous cells into the blood.[15] These promising results were all obtained in animal experiments, however, and by 1999 tests of the drugs in human patients were just beginning.

The discovery that a rare genetic disease called adenosine deaminase (ADA) deficiency destroys white blood cells eventually led to a treatment for an uncommon type of leukemia called hairy-cell leukemia. (Its name comes from the fine, hairlike projections on cells in the blood and bone marrow.) In 1977, Dr. Dennis Carson, a medical researcher at Scripps Clinic and Research Foundation in La Jolla, California, found that in children with ADA deficiency, toxic chemicals build up in the lymphocytes and eventually kill them, leaving the children defenseless against attack by disease germs. People with leukemia have the opposite problem—white cells become abnormal and multiply uncontrollably. Dr. Carson thought that toxins like those in ADA deficiency might be able to kill the leukemic cells.

Searching the scientific literature, he found twenty-five chemicals that resembled the toxins that kill lymphocytes in ADA deficiency. With the help of one laboratory technician, he made these chemicals and tested each one on tumor cells growing in laboratory cultures. "It was a tremendous amount of work," said Dr. Carson, but it paid off. In a test tube of blood treated with one of the substances, cladribine, the lymphocytes were killed while other blood cells were unaffected. In later tests, cladribine produced complete remission in 85

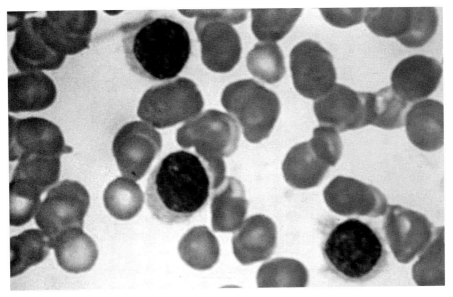

This slide shows the cells of hairy-cell leukemia.

percent of human patients with hairy-cell leukemia. It killed only the out-of-control lymphocytes, without harming normal body cells that also divide frequently, such as those in the skin and hair.[16] Cladribine was later found to be effective in some other types of leukemia and also against multiple sclerosis, but it is not a perfect "magic bullet." This drug is rather toxic, producing damage to normal bone marrow cells as well as diseased cells.

The new genetic technologies have provided a way to produce a real, made-to-order "magic bullet" that specifically targets leukemia-causing viruses. In experiments on mice, researchers at Ohio University stopped leukemia viruses from infecting cells. The leukemia viruses carry their genetic

Souvenir of Paris

Hematologist (a doctor or researcher who specializes in diseases of the blood) Laurent Degos was studying the effects of retinoic acid on leukemia in Paris in 1985 when a colleague from Shanghai, Wang Zhen-Yi, came to visit. Dr. Degos reasoned that retinoic acid, which is closely related to vitamin A, works on acne by speeding up the maturation of skin cells, so that mature, inflamed cells die off and are replaced more quickly by healthy new ones. Could this chemical also help in leukemia, a disease in which white blood cells fail to mature?

In test-tube experiments, Dr. Degos found that all-trans, a synthetic form of retinoic acid, did indeed cause some leukemic cells to mature and die off. After observing these experiments, Dr. Wang returned to Shanghai, where all-trans could be bought easily in local drugstores. He tried it on his patients with promyelocytic leukemia, the type of leukemia against which the drug was most effective in the test tube, and twenty-three out of twenty-four of these patients went into complete remission.

Dr. Degos visited China in 1987 and brought back a supply of all-trans pills, which were not as readily available in the West. Within three months, 75 percent of his patients were in remission. In 1989 researchers at Memorial Sloan-Kettering Cancer Center in New York invited Dr. Degos for a visit. Soon the American researchers were testing tretinoin, a form of retinoic acid, on their patients, too. The drug was so effective that it was approved by the FDA in 1995 for the treatment of acute promyelocytic leukemia, in spite of some potentially dangerous side effects.[17]

information on RNA, a type of genetic material, which then directs infected cells to produce DNA copies—genes that direct the production of new virus particles that can infect other cells. The researchers caused the mouse cells to make antisense RNA, an exact mirror image of a portion of the virus's RNA that is involved in a key step in the virus reproduction. The antisense RNA stuck to the virus gene like a Band-Aid®, preventing it from working. New virus particles were produced, but now they lacked part of their genetic instructions and could not infect other cells. In the mouse experiments, the antisense RNA was used to treat embryos that grew into mice resistant to leukemia. The researchers

Dr. Paolo Borges (right) and his assistant inject leukemia cells into mice at Jackson Memorial Laboratory in Bar Harbor, Maine. Experiments on mice lead the way to effective treatments for people.

pointed out that although such a treatment would not be used on humans, gene therapy techniques could be used to introduce antisense RNA into bone marrow stem cells. These marrow cells would then multiply and repopulate the blood-forming tissues, making people resistant to infection by leukemia viruses.[18]

Antisense RNA can be effective not only against cancer viruses, but also against working genes in leukemic cells. Researchers have already found a number of genes associated with various types of leukemia, and these genes are potential targets for antisense drugs.[19] Atlantic Pharmaceuticals, for example, announced late in 1998 that its researchers had developed an antisense drug that can suppress the growth of chronic myelogenous leukemia (CML) cells. One of the authors of the study, Dr. Robert H. Silverman, noted that the new drug prevents the formation of a protein that helps to trigger CML. "As a result," he stated, "we believe we can suppress the growth of CML cells from patients' bone marrow. The potential, and hope, is that we may one day be able to selectively purge bone marrow of the leukemia cells."[20]

Just one year later, researchers had taken a giant step toward fulfilling that potential. Late in 1999, UCLA researcher Dr. Charles Sawyers announced at an AMA conference that patients with CML taking an antisense drug developed by the pharmaceutical company Novartis had seen their blood counts return to normal. The drug, STI-571, targets the defect in the "Philadelphia chromosome" responsible for producing an abnormal enzyme that stimulates runaway growth of white blood cells. Since this enzyme is found only in leukemia cells, there are few side effects. The patients' bodies produced healthy new white blood cells, and in some cases the defective chromosome actually disappeared after several months of taking the drug. "That is the real home run," Dr. Sawyers says.[21]

A second phase of testing, begun in the autumn of 1999, included patients with more advanced cases of CML, as well as patients with acute lymphocytic leukemia who tested positive for the Philadelphia chromosome. The researchers believe that similar drugs may work for other kinds of cancer.

With approaches such as these under active development in laboratories around the world, we can look forward to the development of many more effective new treatments for leukemia. As the mysteries of human genetic material are revealed and genetic technologies are perfected, scientists may someday even be able to "reengineer" our bodies and those of our descendants to make them leukemia-proof—the ultimate protection against this deadly disease.

Q & A

Q. My best friend was just diagnosed with leukemia, and my mom says I shouldn't play with him because I might catch it. Is this true?

A. Your mom doesn't have all the latest information. Leukemia is not contagious. You can't catch it by touching someone who has it, breathing the same air, or even sharing food or clothing.

Q. My grandfather died of leukemia. Does that mean it runs in my family and I'm going to get it, too?

A. No, leukemia is not hereditary. It is usually caused by conditions in the environment like chemicals or radiation.

Q. You say leukemia isn't hereditary, but I read that scientists have found leukemia genes. What's the story here?

A. Each of the cells in your body has a complete set of genes, which you inherited from your mother and father. But things can happen to damage the genes after you were born, including changes that could lead to leukemia. So even though genes are involved, the disease is not inherited; and if you have it, you won't necessarily pass it on to your own children.

Q. My little brother has been sick a lot lately, and the doctor just told us he has leukemia. Is he going to die?

A. Maybe, but it's getting less likely all the time. Treatments for childhood leukemias are very effective these days, and most children recover.

Q. I've been feeling tired all the time lately. How can I tell if I have leukemia?

A. Leukemia can make you feel tired, but so can a lot of other things, like anemia, mononucleosis, or not getting enough sleep. Do you have any other symptoms, such as frequent illnesses, bruises on your skin when you can't remember getting bumped, or bleeding a lot from little cuts? If so, talk to your doctor, who may want to run some tests.

Q. The doctor says I need to get a test called a spinal tap. I've heard it's very, very painful. Do I have to?

A. You may have a bad headache and nausea after a spinal tap, but it can give important information about your condition that is necessary for working out the best treatment. You can have an easier time if you can relax. Picture a pretty scene or think about something pleasant to take your mind off the test.

Q. Will I lose all my hair if I have chemotherapy? If I do, will it ever grow back?

A. The cells that form your hair divide very rapidly, much like leukemia cells, so the drugs may kill them, too. But after the chemotherapy is finished, your hair will all grow back.

Q. Does it hurt to be a bone marrow donor?

A. A little, but drugs are used to make the spot numb when the needle is inserted, and the pain doesn't last long.

Q. Could I get AIDS from a bone marrow transplant?

A. It's possible, but very unlikely. The marrow used for the transplant is carefully tested for HIV, hepatitis viruses, and other disease germs.

Leukemia Timeline

1827—Alfred Velpeau (France) described a leukemia case for the first time.

1839—Doctors Barth and Donne (France) observed leukemia cases.

1845—David Craigie and John Hughes Bennett (Scotland) reported on leukemia cases; Rudolf Virchow (Germany) described a leukemia case and named the disease *weisses blut* ("white blood").

1847—Virchow changed the name of the disease to leukemia.

1861—D. Biermer (Germany) described leukemia in a child for the first time.

1890—Paul Ehrlich (Germany) distinguished among types of white blood cells and found that when myeloid cells from the bone marrow become abnormal, they accumulate in the liver and spleen.

1903—Marie and Pierre Curie (France) won a Nobel Prize for discovery of the radioactive elements radium and polonium.

1919—Autopsy reports on soldiers poisoned by mustard gas in World War I showed it damaged the bone marrow and lymph nodes.

1934—Marie Curie died of leukemia.

1942—United States researchers used nitrogen mustard as chemotherapy for lymphoma.

1948—United States researchers used folic acid derivatives in chemotherapy of acute leukemia.

1968—The first bone marrow transplant was performed at the University of Minnesota.

1990—United States researchers demonstrated that a damaged gene located on chromosome 22 causes chronic myelogenous leukemia.

1992—Researchers in the United States reported that an abnormal gene on chromosome 11 can lead to several common kinds of leukemia; the first public cord blood bank was set up at the New York Blood Center.

1995—The FDA approved tretinoin for treatment of acute promyelocytic leukemia—the first leukemia treatment using a drug stimulating cell maturation.

1998—Researchers in Israel and Italy reported on a new technique for eliminating the graft-versus-host reaction by removing T lymphocytes from bone marrow stem cells used for transplants; Atlantic Pharmaceuticals announced the development of an antisense drug for treatment of chronic myelogenous leukemia.

1999—Remission of CML was achieved by treatment with an antisense drug targeting the defect in the Philadelphia chromosome that produces a leukemia-stimulating enzyme.

Glossary

acute—pertaining to a severe illness that progresses rapidly.

alkaloids—drugs derived from plants, which interrupt cell division, stopping the reproduction of cancer cells.

alkylating agents—drugs that kill cancer cells by interfering with DNA and RNA, preventing the cells from dividing.

allogeneic BMT—transplantation of healthy bone marrow from a donor into a leukemia patient.

ALL—acute lymphocytic leukemia.

AML—acute myelogenous leukemia; also called myelocytic.

anemia—a condition in which the number of red blood cells is sharply reduced, with symptoms (tiredness, weakness) due to the reduced oxygen-carrying capacity.

angiogenesis—the formation of new blood vessels.

angiostatin—byproduct of cancerous tumors that prevents new tumor growth.

antibiotics—drugs that kill bacteria or block the reproduction of cancer cells.

antimetabolites—drugs that replace important cell nutrients such as folic acid with similar (but not useful) substances.

antisense RNA—a mirror image of a segment of RNA, which binds to it and prevents it from working in protein synthesis.

aspiration—removal of a fluid through a hollow needle.

autologous BMT—transplantation of a patient's own bone marrow, which has been removed and treated to free it of leukemic cells.

autopsy—a postmortem (after death) examination of a body to determine the cause of death.

biopsy—the removal of a small sample of living tissue for microscopic examination to establish a diagnosis or follow the course of a disease.

blasts—immature white blood cells.

bone marrow—spongy material found inside the cavities of large bones, in which red and white blood cells and platelets are formed.

bone marrow biopsy—collection and analysis of a sample of bone marrow cells.

bone marrow transplantation (BMT)—replacement of a leukemia patient's bone marrow with healthy marrow from a compatible donor.

calcination—burning of radioactive wastes to a dry powder.

capillaries—the smallest blood vessels, which carry oxygen and nutrients to all the body cells and remove their waste products.

carcinogen—a cancer-causing chemical or substance.

CBC (complete blood count)—a test that measures the total numbers of red and white blood cells and platelets in the blood.

chemotherapy—the use of drugs ("chemicals") to treat diseases by killing invading germs or cancerous cells or by stopping their growth and reproduction.

chronic—pertaining to a long-term illness (usually less severe than an acute illness).

circulatory system—the heart and blood vessels.

CLL—chronic lymphocytic leukemia.

CML—chronic myelogenous leukemia.

consolidation therapy—the second stage of chemotherapy, started after the patient is in remission; a new combination of drugs is used to kill any remaining leukemic cells.

cord blood—blood drained from the umbilical cord and placenta after birth.

differential white blood cell count—examination of a stained blood sample to determine the percentages of the different types of white blood cells.

endostatin—substance produced by lining of blood vessels, which stops the formation of new blood vessels to tumors.

enzymes—proteins that affect chemical reactions; used in leukemia treatment to prevent reproduction of cancer cells by stopping their protein production.

erythroblasts—immature red blood cells.

erythrocytes—mature red blood cells.

graft-versus-host disease (GVHD)—illness due to an attack on the recipient's body by immune system cells in a donor transplant whose HLA antigens do not match well enough.

granulocytes—the most common white blood cells, which seek out and destroy disease germs.

hematocrit—the volume of red blood cells as a percentage of the volume of a blood sample.

hematologist—a specialist in blood cells and blood-forming tissues.

hemoglobin—a red-colored protein found in red blood cells; it helps to carry oxygen to the body cells and to carry away the cells' carbon dioxide wastes.

HLA (human leukocyte-associated antigens)—proteins on the surface of white blood cells that act as signals for distinguishing "self" cells from foreign cells.

hormones—chemicals that control and coordinate cell activities; used in leukemia treatment to slow cell growth.

HTLV (human T-cell leukemia/lymphoma virus)—a virus that attacks T cells (a type of lymphocytes) and causes a rare form of leukemia.

immune system—the body's defenses against invading germs or foreign cells and tissues.

induction therapy—the first stage of chemotherapy, in which large doses of anticancer drugs are used to kill as many leukemic cells as possible.

leukemia—a cancer of the blood-forming tissues, in which abnormal white blood cells multiply uncontrollably.

leukocytes—mature white blood cells.

lymph nodes—masses of glandlike tissue found along the lymph vessels, especially in the neck, groin, and armpits.

lymphatic system—a network of vessels that return lymph (fluid drained from the tissues after leaking out of blood capillaries) to the circulatory system.

lymphoblasts—immature lymphocytes.

lymphocytes—white blood cells found in large numbers in lymph nodes and other lymphoid tissues; different kinds participate in immune responses by recognizing and attacking foreign invaders, producing antibodies, or aiding in their production.

lymphocytic leukemia—leukemia of the lymphoid organs with overproduction of immature lymphocytes; also called lymphoblastic, lymphatic, or lyphoid leukemia.

lymphoma—a cancer of the lymph nodes.

macrophages—large white blood cells that develop from monocytes and attack and eat invading germs.

maintenance therapy—the third stage of chemotherapy, in which low doses of drugs are taken for several years to prevent relapse.

monoblasts—immature white blood cells that can develop into monocytes and macrophages.

monocytes—a type of white blood cell that attacks and eats invading germs.

myeloblasts—immature myelocytes.

myelocytes—bone marrow cells, especially those that develop into granulocytes.

myelocytic leukemia—leukemia of the bone marrow, with an overproduction of immature granulocytes; also called myeloblastic, myeloid, myelogenous, or granulocytic leukemia.

myeloid cells—white blood cells produced in the bone marrow.

neutrophils—a type of granulocyte; the most numerous of the white blood cells.

placenta—a blood-filled organ in the womb of a pregnant woman, through which her body supplies the developing baby with nourishment.

platelets—see *thrombocytes.*

purging—destroying any cancer cells remaining in autologous bone marrow for a transplant.

radiation therapy—the use of high doses of X rays (or other radiations) to kill cancer cells deep inside the body; also called radiotherapy.

rejection—destruction of a transplanted organ or tissue that the recipient's immune system has recognized as foreign.

relapse—return (recurrence) of an illness.

remission—a lessening or disappearance of disease symptoms and signs.

spinal tap—collection of a sample of cerebrospinal fluid (CSF) with a hollow needle inserted in the gap between two vertebrae; also called lumbar puncture.

stem cells—primitive blood-forming cells that can produce whatever kind of blood cells are needed.

syngeneic BMT—transplantation of bone marrow from an identical twin.

thrombocytes—disk-shaped particles that cause blood to form clots to stop bleeding; also called platelets.

vasectomy—a surgical procedure intended to induce sterility in males.

vitrification—sealing of radioactive wastes into a stable, solid glass.

For More Information

Leukemia Organizations:

American Cancer Society
1599 Clifton Road, NE
Atlanta, GA 30329
404-320-3333

Leukemia Society of America
National Office
600 Third Avenue
New York, NY 10016
212-573-8484
800-955-4LSA
http://www.leukemia.org/hm_11s

National Cancer Institute
Office of Cancer Communications
Bethesda, MD 20892
800-4-CANCER

National Institutes of Health
9000 Rockville Pike
Bethesda, MD 20205
301-763-7083

Bone Marrow Organizations:

American Bone Marrow Donor Registry
800-745-2452
http://www.abmdr.org

Caitlin Raymond International Registry
University of Massachusetts Medical Center
53 Lake Avenue North
Worcester, MA 01655
508-792-8969
http://www.crir.org

National Marrow Donor Program
3433 Broadway Street NE
Suite 400
Minneapolis, MN 55413-1762
800-MARROW-2
http://www.Marrow.org

New York Cord Blood Registry
The Fred H. Allen Laboratory of Immunogenetics
The New York Blood Center
310 East 67th Street
New York, NY 10021
212-570-3230
e-mail: stem@nybc.org

Chapter Notes

Chapter 1. Blood Cells Gone Wild

1. Shelley Bruce, "Broadway's Former 'Annie' Scores Another Triumph by Overcoming Leukemia," *People Weekly*, May 3, 1982, pp. 139–141.

Chapter 2. Leukemia in History

1. Florence Reynal, "Marie Curie: A Nobel Prize Pioneer at the Panthéon," <http://www.france.diplomatie.fr/label_france/ENGLISH/SCIENCES/CURIE/marie.html> (December 21, 1999).

2. Ibid.

3. "Marie Curie—A Biographical Insight," <http://zen.suderland.ac.uk/~hb5hco/marie.htm> (December 3, 1998).

4. John Laszlo, *The Cure of Childhood Leukemia: Into the Age of Miracles* (New Brunswick, N.J.: Rutgers University Press, 1996), pp. 12–13.

5. Ibid., p. 13.

6. Ibid., pp. 13–14.

7. Ibid., pp. 14–15.

8. Laszlo, p. 17.

9. Ibid.

10. Ibid., p. 20.

11. Sheila T. Callender, *Blood Disorders: The Facts* (New York: Oxford University Press, 1985), p. 105.

12. Children's Cancer Research Fund, "Blood and Marrow Transplantation," 1997, <http://www.childrenscancer.com/research/res_bmt.html> (December 21, 1999).

Chapter 3. What Is Leukemia?

1. John Laszlo, *The Cure of Childhood Leukemia: Into the Age of Miracles* (New Brunswick, N.J.: Rutgers University Press), 1996, pp. 7–9.

2. Leukemia Society of America, "Leukemia, Lymphomas, & Myeloma," <http://www.leukemia.org/docs/leuk_rel/fc_leukemia.html> (December 21, 1999).

3. Nancy Keene, *Childhood Leukemia: A Guide for Families, Friends, and Caregivers* (Sebastopol, Calif.: O'Reilly, 1997), p. 22.

4. Leukemia Society of America, *What Everyone Should Know About Leukemia,* pamphlet, November 1998, p. 9.

5. Ernest J. Sternglass, "The Hidden Tragedy of Hiroshima," from *Secret Fallout: Low Level Radiation from Hiroshima to Three Mile Island,* 1981, <http://www.ratical.org/radiation/SecretFallout/SFchp6.html> (January 10, 2000).

6. Sandy Rovner, "Study Linking Hot Dogs to Child Cancer Called Provocative," *The Courier-News* (Bridgewater, N.J.), July 3, 1994, p. B-6.

7. Leukaemia Research Fund, "Leukaemia and the Related Diseases," <http://www.leukaemia.demon.co.uk/leuk.htm#normal> (December 21, 1999); Miles W. Cloyd, "Human Retroviruses," <http://gsbs.utmb.edu/microbook/ch062.htm> (December 21, 1999).

8. National Childhood Cancer Foundation, "Genetic Etiology of Acute Leukemia in Down Syndrome (CCG Protocol: B957)," 1996, <http://www.nccf.org/nccf/cancer/protocol/B957.htm> (January 19, 2000).

9. Leukemia Society of America, Chronic Myelogenous Leukemia, pamphlet, December 1997, p. 6—can also be found online at <http://www.leukemia.org/docs/pub_media/cml/index.html> (December 21, 1999).

10. Keene, p. 22.

11. "Research Studies Leukemia Drugs in Children with Down Syndrome: When One Disease Helps Fight Another," *Karmanos News*, April 15, 1996, <http://www.karmanos.org/ news13.html> (December 21, 1999).

12. Geralyn and Craig Gaes, and Philip Bashe, *You Don't Have to Die: One Family's Guide to Surviving Childhood Cancer* (New York: Villard Books, 1992), pp. 36–37.

13. Keene, pp. 25–33.

Chapter 4. Diagnosing Leukemia

1. Katie McCabe, "Window of Hope," *Reader's Digest*, July 1992, pp. 79–91, 189–210.

2. National Cancer Institute, "Leukemia," <http://cancernet. nci.nih.gov/young_people/yngleukemia.html> (December 21, 1999).

3. KidsHealth.org, "Blood Tests: CBC (Complete Blood Count)," 1996, <http://kidshealth.org/parent/healthy/labtests/ labtest4.html> (December 21, 1999).

4. Leukaemia Research Fund, "Leukaemia and the Related Diseases," <http://www.leukaemia.demon.co.uk/leuk. htm#normal> (December 21, 1999).

5. American Cancer Society, "How Is Childhood Leukemia Diagnosed," p. 2, <http://www3.cancer.org/cancerinfo/main_cont. asp?st=ds&ct=24> (December 21, 1999).

6. Nancy Keene, *Childhood Leukemia: A Guide for Families, Friends, and Caregivers* (Sebastopol, Calif.: O'Reilly, 1997), p. 52.

7. William H. Allen, "The Battle Against Leukemia," *The World Book Health and Medical Annual 1994* (Chicago: World Book, Inc., 1994), pp. 207–208.

8. Keene, p. 54.

9. Geralyn and Craig Gaes, and Bashe, Philip, *You Don't Have to Die: One Family's Guide to Surviving Childhood Cancer* (New York: Villard Books, 1992), p. 38.

Chapter 5. Treating Leukemia

1. Marjorie Rosen & Michael Arkush, "The Game of His Life," *People*, December 4, 1995, pp. 133–135.

2. Leukemia Society of America, "Leukemia, Lymphomas, & Myeloma," <http://www.leukemia.org/docs/leuk_rel/fc_leukemia. html> (December 21, 1999).

3. Mark Terenzi, "Life-Saving Donations," *The Courier-News* (Bridgewater, N.J.), March 4, 1999, Strictly Hunterdon section, p. 1.

4. Nancy Keene, *Childhood Leukemia: A Guide for Families, Friends, and Caregivers* (Sebastopol, Calif.: O'Reilly, 1997), pp. 58–60.

5. CancerHelp UK, "Questions and Answers: Chemotherapy," November 14, 1997, <http://medweb.bham.ac.uk/cancerhelp/ public/qanda/chemo/chemical.html> (December 21, 1999).

6. Keene, pp. 26–28.

7. CancerHelp UK, "Questions and Answers: Chemotherapy."

8. Keene, p. 174.

9. Ibid., pp. 209–210.

10. Ibid., pp. 229–230.

11. Ibid., p. 400.

12. "The Nuts and Bolts of Bone Marrow Transplants," Chapter 1 of *Bone Marrow Transplants—A Basic Book for Patients*, <http://www. oncolink.upenn.edu/specialty/med_onc/bmt_1.html> (December 21, 1999).

13. Ibid.

14. Childhood Leukemia Foundation, "CLF's Late Breaking News," 1996, p. 2, <http://www.clf4kids.com/index2.html> (December 3, 1998).

Chapter 6. Preventing Leukemia

1. Eleanor Coerr, *Sadako and the Thousand Paper Cranes* (New York: Bantam Doubleday Dell Books for Young Readers, 1977), pp. 1–64.

2. U.S. Arms Control and Disarmament Agency, "Comprehensive Test Ban Treaty," <http://www.peacenet.org/disarm/ctbt.html> (December 21, 1999); U.S. Arms Control and Disarmament Agency, "Events and Campaigns: Nuclear Testing," <http://www.peacenet.org/disarm/testing.html> (December 21, 1999).

3. "Chernobyl—First Results In," <http://whyfiles.news.wisc.edu/020radiation/chern2.html> (December 21, 1999); Dr. K. F. Baverstock from the World Health Organization, "The Chernobyl Accident—Health Effects," April 28, 1995, <http://www.uilondon.org/whobab.htm> (December 21, 1999).

4. "Research and New Advancements in Nuclear Waste Technology," <http://starfire.ne.uiuc.edu/ne201/course/old_web_projects/chang/nuce201d.html>; Peter Kish Dill of University of Berkeley, Calif., "Radioactive Waste," <http://www.neu.Berkeley.edu/thyd/ne161/pdill/waste.html#Radioactivity> (December 21, 1999).

5. Phil Brown, "When the Public Knows Better: Popular Epidemiology Challenges the System," *Environment*, October 1993, pp. 16–17.

6. Daniel D. Kennedy, "Stalking Woburn's Mystery Killer," from *MetroNorth Magazine*, Winter 1989–1990, <http://www2.shore.net/~dkennedy/woburn_mit.html> (December 21, 1999).

Chapter 7. Leukemia and Society

1. "Anissa Ayala: Thriving on a Sister's Gift of Love—and Life," *People*, November 28, 1994, p. 116.

2. Lawrence Elliott, "A Healing Birth," *Reader's Digest*, June 1997, p. 243.

3. Lance Morrow, "When One Body Can Save Another," *Time*, June 17, 1991, pp. 54–61.

4. Gina Kolata, "More Babies Being Born to Be Donors of Tissue," *The New York Times*, June 4, 1991, p. A1.

5. Ibid.

6. Morrow, pp. 54–61.

7. Nancy Gibbs, "The Gift of Life—Or Else," *Time*, September 10, 1990, p. 70.

8. Katie McCabe, "Window of Hope," *Reader's Digest*, July 1992, pp. 91, 189–207.

9. Ibid., pp. 207–210.

10. Marjorie Rosen and Michael Arkush, "The Game of His Life," *People*, December 4, 1995, pp. 133–135.

Chapter 8. Leukemia and the Future

1. Susan Fenelon Kerr, "Umbilical Cord Program Banks on Donors," *The Star-Ledger* (Newark, N.J.), April 5, 1998, Section 2, p. 13.

2. Pablo Rubinstein et al., "Outcomes among 562 Recipients of Placental-Blood Transplants from Unrelated Donors," *The New England Journal of Medicine*, November 26, 1998, pp. 1565–1577.

3. Linda A. Johnson, "Blood from Umbilical Cords Might Save Cancer Victims," *The Courier-News* (Bridgewater, N.J.), November 26, 1998, p. A-24.

4. Denise Grady, "Umbilical Cord May Be Lifeline in Marrow Cases, *The New York Times*, November 26, 1998, p. A36.

5. Kerr, p. 13.

6. Ibid.

7. Christine Gorman, "Miracle Blood," *Time*, December 21, 1998, p. 93.

8. Ibid.

9. Grady, p. A36.

10. Gorman, p. 93.

11. Grady, p. A36.

12. Franco Aversa et al., "Treatment of High-Risk Acute Leukemia with T-Cell-Depleted Stem Cells from Related Donors with One Fully Mismatched HLA Haplotype," *The New England Journal of Medicine*, October 22, 1998, pp. 1186–1193.

13. Jon J. van Rood, "The Quest for a Bone Marrow Donor—Optimal or Maximal HLA Matching?" *The New England Journal of Medicine*, October 22, 1998, p. 1238.

14. Dana-Farber Cancer Institute, press release, June 1999, "New Technique Holds Promise of Creating Universal Donor Pool for Transplantation," <http://www.dfci.harvard.edu/site1/news/NS4/donorpool.asp> (July 21, 1999).

15. Gina Kolata, "A Cautious Awe Greets Drugs That Eradicate Tumors in Mice," *The New York Times*, May 3, 1998, pp. 1, 34.

16. Kathy A. Fackelmann, "Traitorous Lymphocytes," *Science News*, June 11, 1994, pp. 378–379.

17. Peter Radetsky, "Reversing Leukemia," *Discover*, July 1991, p. 24.

18. Deborah Erickson, "Molecular Trickster," *Scientific American*, July 1991, p. 26.

19. Phyllida Brown, "Gene Jam Holds Hope for Leukaemia Therapy," *New Scientist*, August 10, 1991, p. 21.

20. Atlantic Pharmaceuticals, "Atlantic Pharmaceuticals Publishes Findings in Top Hematology Journal Showing That Compound Utilizing Company's 25A Antisense Technology Has Potential to Inhibit Chronic Myelogenous Leukemia," press release, November 30, 1998, <http://www.atlan.com/p113098blood.htm> (January 18, 2000).

21. "Leukemia-Fighting Drug Produces Dramatic Results in Clinical Trials," *Doctor's Guide*, October 26, 1999, <http://www.pslgroup.com/dg/13EA9A.htm> (January 13, 2000).

Further Reading

Books

Coerr, Eleanor. *Sadako and the Thousand Paper Cranes.* New York: G. P. Putnam's Sons, 1977.

Huegel, Kelly. *Young People & Chronic Illness: True Stories, Help, and Hope.* Minneapolis, Minn.: Free Spirit Publishing, Incorporated, 1998.

Keene, Nancy. *Childhood Leukemia: A Guide for Families, Friends, and Caregivers.* Sebastopol, Calif.: O'Reilly and Associates, 1997.

Peacock, Judith. *Leukemia.* Mankato, Minn.: Capstone Press, 1999.

Roff, Sue R. *Hotspots: The Legacy of Hiroshima and Nagasaki.* New York: Cassell Academic, 1995.

Siegel, Dorothy Schainman and David E. Newton. *Leukemia.* New York: Franklin Watts, 1994.

Smedley, Jack L. *The Journey Back: A Survivor's Guide to Leukemia.* Baden, Penn.: Rainbow's End Company, 1996.

Articles

Allen, William H., "The Battle Against Leukemia," *The World Book Health and Medical Annual 1994,* pp. 201–215.

Brown, Phil, "When the Public Knows Better," *Environment,* October 1993, pp. 16–40.

Elliott, Lawrence. "A Healing Birth," *Reader's Digest,* June 1997, pp. 147–152, 231–258.

Kline, Ronald. "New Marrow for Old," *Technology Review*, November/December 1993, pp. 43–49.

Kolata, Gina. "More Babies Being Born To Be Donors of Tissue," *The New York Times*, June 4, 1991, pp. A1, C3.

McCabe, Katie. "Window of Hope," *Reader's Digest*, July 1992, pp. 79–91, 189–210.

————. "Sweet Hope," *Reader's Digest*, November 1993, pp. 23–32.

Morrow, Lance. "When One Body Can Save Another," *Time*, June 17, 1991, pp. 54–61.

Taylor, Dick and David Wilkie. "Drawing the Line with Leukaemia," *New Scientist*, July 21, 1988, pp. 53–56.

Younger, James. "Nuclear Plant Cleared in Leukemia Cluster," *The New York Times*, March 3, 1994, pp. C1, C13.

Internet Resources

"CancerNet: Information for Health Professionals, Patients and the Public," <http://cancernet.nci.nih.gov> (site maintained by the National Cancer Institute).

"Childhood Leukemia FAQ," <http://patientcenters.com> (questions and answers about childhood leukemia based on the book by Nancy Keene).

"Cranes for Peace," <http://www.he.net/~sparker/cranes.html> (resource center for Sadako-related projects).

Harr, Jonathan, "A Civil Action," <http://www.randomhouse.com/vintage/read/civilaction>.

"Leukaemia and the Related Diseases," <http://dspace.dial.pipex.com/lrf-/> (informational booklets on Normal Blood Cell Production, the Conditions, the Causes, Diagnosis, Classification and Staging, and Treatment).

"Leukemia World," <http://www.worldmedic.com/leukemia. htm> (information and links for: Living with Leukemia, Know About Leukemia, Treating Leukemia, Leukemia and Genetics, Leukemia Information, and Causes of Leukemia).

"National Marrow Donor Program," <http://www.marrow.org> (patient and donor information, news, and donor and patient stories).

"The Nuts and Bolts of Bone Marrow Transplants," <http:// oncolink.upenn.edu/specialty/med_onc/bmt/> (reprint from the BMT Handbook).

"Sadako and the Thousand Paper Cranes," <http://www. sadako.org/SadakoHome.htm> (The Sadako Home Page, sponsored by songwriter Michiko and the World Peace Project for Children.)

The Sadako Film Project, "The Story of Sadako," 1997, <http://www.sadako.com/story.html>.

Sadako Peace Club for Children, "The Sadako Story," 1997, <http://www.sadakostory.org/peaceclub.htm>.

"Toxic Legacy: Hazardous Waste and the Lessons of Woburn, Massachusetts," <http://www2.shore.net/~dkennedy/ woburn.html> (articles by Dan Kennedy).

Index